Academic English
EAP Course Book & Syllabus
Including IELTS Practice

By Robert Chalmers

Published by
R.A.Chalmers.
Publishing & Programming
www.chalmers.com.au

The right of Robert Chalmers. MA(TESOL), BA, GrdDipTch, DipJourn, has been identified
as authyor of this Work has been asserted by her in accordance with the Copyright,Designs
and Patients Act 1988.
First Published 2011
ISBN: 978-0-9807985-3-1

Printed by Lulu.com

Cover design by Robert Chalmers

Table of Contents

Introduction i

    To the teacher iii

    To the Distance Education student iv

  To all students iv

Section 1: Student English 1

    What you can expect. 1

    Study Guide 2

Section Two: EAP 14

Module 1 Customs 15

    Module Overview 15

    Module Objectives 16

    Learning resources 16

    Introductory comment 16

      Activity: Following Maps & Directions 18

    Lesson focus 18

    1.1   Reading 18

    1.2   Speaking 18

    1.3   Writing 20

    Key - Stereotypes in multicultural Europe 23

    Key references for further study 24

    References 24

Module 2 Trade 25

    Module Overview 25

    Module Objectives 26

    Learning resources 26

    Introductory comment 26

      Activity: Interviews & Surveys 28

    2.1 Trade: Core Vocabulary 28

    Key references for further study 37

    References 37

Module 3 Demography 38

    Module Overview 38

    Module Objectives 39

    Learning resources 39

Introductory comment 39

Key references for further study 43

References 43

Module 4 Energy 44

    Module Overview 44

    Module Objectives 45

    Learning resources 45

    Introductory comment 45

    Key references for further study 53

    References 54

Module 5 Communication 55

    Module Overview 55

    Module Objectives 56

    Learning resources 56

    Introductory comment 56

    Key references for further study 66

    References 66

Module 6 Politics 67

    Module Overview 67

    Module Objectives 68

    Learning resources 68

    Introductory comment 68

    Key references for further study 75

    References 75

Module 7 Media 76

    Module Overview 76

    Module Objectives 77

    Learning resources 77

    Introductory comment 77

    Key references for further study 85

    References 85

Module 8 Art 86

    Module Overview 86

    Module Objectives 87

    Learning resources 87

    Introductory comment 87

Key references for further study 91

References 91

Module 9 Architecture 92

Module Overview 92

Module Objectives 93

Learning resources 93

Introductory comment 93

Key references for further study 99

References 99

Module 10 Indigenous People 100

Module Overview 100

Module Objectives 101

Learning resources 101

Introductory comment 101

Key references for further study 108

References 108

Module 11 Landscapes 109

Module Overview (Extension) 109

Module Objectives 110

Learning resources 110

Introductory comment 110

Key references for further study 118

References 118

Module 12 Landscapes 119

Module Overview (Extension) 119

Module Objectives 120

Learning resources 120

Introductory comment 120

Key references for further study 127

References 127

EAP Assessment 128

Full Text Book Reference List 129

Introduction

This course book has been designed for the International Student wishing to study Academic English and seeking to achieve a level that will gain Direct Entry into a college or university of choice in a Western country like Australia, the United Kingdom, or the United States of America.

It is also designed for students who wish to bring their level of English up to an acceptable International Standard, but not necessarily wishing to go overseas for further study. The lesson structure has been designed by a team of professional IELTS and Academic English teachers, and is enhanced by a set of published resources readily available in most countries of the world.

The book has been written for use without a teacher, as well as in the class room. Thus it suits ideally the Distance Education scenario, as well as the formal teacher-student classroom arrangement.

Level
The book is intended mainly for upper intermediate students. Students who have already studied the basics of English and now wish to advance their skills to genuine levels of competency. It is designed for students wishing to gain Direct Entry into a College or University course or program.
This course work is designed to take a student who has achieved an intermediate level of English to a level of confidence and ability that will allow them to begin their course work with confidence, needing no further time in overseas English Language programs. It is designed to bring a student up to a solid Level 6 to 6.5 on the IELTS scale.

This book is *not* suitable for elementary learners.

How the book is organised
There are 12 modules in the book. Each module represents one week of a full time ESL class, of 5 hours per day, 4 days a week for 12 weeks, including two testing weeks.
Each module is theme based, as is standard practice with IELTS testing and learning, as well as having English usage patterns found in every day usage. The modules include the four macro skill areas, of Reading, Writing, Speaking and Listening, and include in-depth Grammar study, and Academic Writing practices.

Each module covers a broad range of material found in the recommended texts, as well as exercises and study guides. The course cannot be undertaken without the recommended texts, and students are encouraged to study material and sources in addition to those prescribed.

Each module is made up in the following format.

- Introduction
- Everyday English
- Academic English
- Grammar Points
- Academic Writing
- Exercises

How to use the book

The units are not in order of difficulty, and you do not have to work through the book from beginning to end. You may find that this is the case in a classroom situation, but even there it is not strictly necessary. Every learner has different needs, and you can use this book to enhance those areas that you feel you may be struggling in.

It is suggested that you use the book in this way initially.
- Use the Contents and/or index to locate points of interest
- If you are not sure which units you need to study, refer to the Study Guide included at the start of this book
- Study the examples and explanations of each days pages you are working on, and work through the work book exercises on a daily basis
- Check your answers after completing the exercises
- If your answers are incorrect, study the references to see what went wrong

Additional Exercises

You will find additional exercises in all of the reference material, as well as in various modules of this course book.

CD Rom

Each resource book comes with a CD Rom. In all the sets contain over 2,000 additional exercises, video clips, audio clips, and test material.

To the teacher

This **Academic English Course Book** is written as both a Self Study book, and a classroom book. Specifically, it is designed for a standard 12 week course, where two of those weeks may be testing weeks. This means that the student has 10 lesson weeks and two revision or exam weeks.

This built in flexibility gives you the teacher the best choices on how to manage delivery so that all the required material is covered.

The book will be of most use at upper-intermediate to advanced levels. You will see that the material covers two central elements.

The first may be called *Every Day English*, to ensure that the student has a wide ranging general knowledge of English speaking society as well as the use of the language in daily life. It is a very rare student indeed who does not have an active social life, and having a good foundation in conversational skills will be most useful in the tutorial or lecture, where often the exchanges are rapid, and cannot wait for someone with marginal levels of understanding of *working English*.

The second is purely Academic English, on two levels. IELTS material resources are used extensively, both because they cover the likely material tested and the usual testing format, and because they embody the necessary Academic blueprints that a student will need at tertiary level. In addition to the IELTS material there are Academic English units, and exercises covering Referencing, Academic Writing and language.

To the Distance Education student

Lessons taken by distance education can seem daunting in the beginning. However this course book has been arranged so that you can progress from one unit to the next over the period of time designated for you studies by the governing institute. For distance education students this is usually from two to three semesters in duration. As you can see, that means if you take the course over three semesters, a total of 36 weeks (one academic year), it gives you only 4 modules per semester of study.

To all students

At first glance, it may seem to some that there is a great deal of material to cover in this Course Book, in a short period of time. It is true. There is actually much more material planned for each day's activities than one student can manage. This is done on purpose, so that you can be selective about what you study.
 It is also true that in the very competitive world of today, only the best succeed. If you can cover as much of the material in each day as is possible, you will achieve Your English Success.

You should obtain the core text books as listed at the end of the Study Guide, and try to obtain access to as much of the other material as possible. All of the text books used and referenced have been selected after rigorous evaluation by many teachers of ESL with years of experience between them, and for the upper-intermediate to advanced student, are most suitable to carry the student to a level of competence that should ensure Direct Entry abilities to the career path of choice.

Section 1: Student English

Including IELTS Practice and Study Guide

This is the complete modularised Student English and IELTS practice component. This should be worked through <u>at the same time</u> as you are studying **Section Two**. Ideally you will study Week 1 from Section One, at the same time as Module One from **Section Two:EAP**
There are 10 core weeks in both components, and the material is designed to progress you through the abilities at the same time.
In a full program, a student should be able to master English for Academic Purposes to a very high standard in the full fifteen weeks of a standard semester.

What you can expect.
Upon completion of these Study Modules, you should expect to be fully able to take part in discourse in a Tertiary Environment – a college or university etc, as well as comfortably manage communications with native English speaking people in your normal daily life. This course is designed to enable the student to achieve Direct Entry to the tertiary course of their choice, up to and including Nursing studies.

In the following Study Guide, NCE stands for <u>New Cutting Edge</u>, one of the required text books, and IELTS stands for <u>IELTS Foundation</u> text book.

In this example, the 5 day week model is used.

Beginning Day 1.

Period
(Day) Text   Workbook   Time   → Approximate time to take on this activity
  1. Pages 6 & 7.   6&7   2h

New Cutting Edge text   New Cutting Edge Workbook Exercises

2. Pages	8 & 9.	8&9	2h	
3. Pages	10 & 11	10&11	2h	... continued from day 1
4. Pages	12 & 13	12&13	2h	
5. Pages	14 & 15	---	2h	

IELTS. Read all about it.
Period
(Day) Text   Workbook   Time

1. Pages	6 & 7.	7	1.5h	
2. Pages	8 & 9.		1.5h	Focus on IELTS Foundation text book, and workbook
3. Pages	10 & 11	8	1.5h	activities from the Teachers Book accompanying the text.
4. Pages	12 & 13		1.5h	The workbook/teachers book activities are optional.
5. Pages	14 & 15	9	1.5h	

Week	Function or Skill	Activities			Notes

Study Guide

| 1 | Core: **All About You.** - Asking and answering questions. *Pronunciation: Auxiliary* verbs. - Present simple and continuous.

Exam Focus: **Reading.** Introducing reading skills. Reading academic texts.

Speaking. Discussing a topic. Expressing a personal opinion.

Grammar. Present simple.

Vocabulary. Word families. Prepositions. Pronunciation. Syllables | Intro: : - A need for vocabulary notebooks. *5 : - The value of newspaper articles. *8

NCE. All about you. Task: Find things in common   Preparation: listening   Task: speaking   Follow up: writing. | | Reading and Speaking: How we really spend our time.

Vocabulary people around you. Words: have, have got.

Key Language Bank. IELTS. Page 140.

Formal and colloquial language. E.g.; to *get* someone to do something. Pronunciation and phonetics chart. Check. * 5. English vocabulary in use. P6 & 7 * 8. English grammar in use. P2 & 3

Irregular verbs: p155. NCE |

Week 1 Activities detail:

NCE. All about you.

Period (Day) Text	Workbook	Time
1. Pages 6 & 7.	6&7	2h
2. Pages 8 & 9.	8&9	2h
3. Pages 10 & 11	10&11	2h
4. Pages 12 & 13	12&13	2h
5. Pages 14 & 15	---	2h

IELTS. Read all about it.

Period (Day) Text	Workbook	Time
1. Pages 6 & 7.	7	1.5h
2. Pages 8 & 9.		1.5h
3. Pages 10 & 11	8	1.5h
4. Pages 12 & 13		1.5h
5. Pages 14 & 15	9	1.5h

| 2 | Core: **Memory.** - Pronunciation - Past simple –ed endings. - used to. - sounding polite. Exam Focus: **Listening.** Letters and sounds. Introducing listening skills.

Speaking. Discussing likes and dislikes. **Writing.** Reading and describing data. Linking expressions. **Grammar.** Frequency adverbs and expressions. | **NCE. Memory.** | | Vocabulary: Remembering and forgetting.

Listening and Speaking: First meetings. A childhood memory. Songs. Reading.

Vocabulary: TV Programmes. Word partners: *Do, give* and *make.*

* 5. English vocabulary in use. P8 & 9 * 8. English grammar in use. P4 & 5 |

Week 2 Activities detail:

NCE. Memory.

Period (Day) Text	Workbook	Time
1. Pages 16 & 17.	14&15	2h
2. Pages 18 & 19.	16&17	2h
3. Pages 20 & 21	18&19	2h
4. Pages 22 & 23	20&21	2h
5. Pages 24 & 25	---	2h

IELTS. Take note.

Period (Day) Text	Workbook	Time
1. Pages 16 & 17.	11	1.5h
2. Pages 18 & 19.		1.5h
3. Pages 20 & 21	12	1.5h
4. Pages 22 & 23		1.5h
5. Pages 24 & 25	13	1.5h
Extension: Pp 26, 27. Review		

Week	Function or Skill	Activities	Notes
3	Language Focus Comparatives and superlatives. Vocabulary Phrases for comparing. Describing towns and cities. Reading: The top 100 places to visit before you die. **Reading.** My worst job, and Service workers are the happiest staff. **Speaking.** Discussing jobs and careers. Job satisfaction. **Grammar.** Past simple. **Vocabulary.** Word partners: pronunciation, word stress.	**Module 3.** **NCE. Around the World.** Period (Day) Text Workbook Time 1. Pages 26 & 27. 22&23 2h 2. Pages 28 & 29. 24&25 2h 3. Pages 30 & 31 26&27 2h 4. Pages 32 & 33 28 --- 2h 5. Pages 34 & 35 --- 2h **IELTS. It goes with the job.** Period (Day) Text Workbook Time 1. Pages 28 & 29 15 1.5h 2. Pages 30 & 31 1.5h 3. Pages 32 & 33 16 1.5h 4. Pages 34 & 35 1.5h 5. Pages 36 & 37 17 1.5h	Task: Design a tour. Preparation: listening Task: speaking Follow up: Writing Further Skills: Real Life. Booking a flight. Key Language Bank. IELTS. Page 140. * 5. English vocabulary in use. P10 & 11 * 8. English grammar in use. P6 & 7

Week	Function or Skill	Activities	Notes
4	**Language Focus:** Present perfect simple. Pronunciation. Strong and weak forms of *have*. *For, since* and *ago* and Present perfect continuous. Pronunciation: Linking. Vocabulary and Writing: Describing life events. Positive characteristics. Wordspot. take. Reading: parallel lives. **Listening.** Letters and sounds International friendship club **Speaking.** Discussing relationships (2) Dealing with difficult questions. **Writing.** Key Skills: Reading and describing data; identifying trends. Paragraphs topic sentences; reference links; supporting sentences. **Grammar.** Articles. Vocabulary. Family tree; right word/wrong word; word families.	**Module 4.** **NCE. Life Stories.** Period (Day) Text Workbook Time 1. Pages 36 & 37 29&30 2h 2. Pages 38 & 39 31&32 2h 3. Pages 40 & 41 33&34 2h 4. Pages 42 & 43 35 --- 2h 5. Pages 44 & 45 --- 2h Consolidation: pp46 & 47 **IELTS. Family Values.** Period (Day) Text Workbook Time 1. Pages 38 & 39 19 1.5h 2. Pages 40 & 41 1.5h 3. Pages 42 & 43 20 1.5h 4. Pages 44 & 45 1.5h 5. Pages 46 & 47 21 1.5h Review. Pages 48 and 49.	Talk about someone you admire. Preparation: listening Task.: speaking Follow up: writing. Writing: a curriculum vitae (*what language is this?) Key Language Bank. IELTS. Page 140. * 5. English vocabulary in use. P12 & 13 * 8. English grammar in use. P8 & 9

Week	Function or Skill	Activities	Notes
5	Language Focus. Future forms Future clauses with *if*, *when*, etc Vocabulary. Work. Reading and Listening. Reading and Vocabulary: Have you got what it takes? Pronunciation: Stressed syllables Listening and Speaking: Doing something different. Song: Manic Monday. Asking for and giving opinions Speaking about global topics. Speculating about future events and their consequences. **Reading**. The Boys of Summer, the Men of Fall. (word Fall) Short answer questions. The Curse of The Referee. Summary completions. **Speaking**. Discussing sports and hobbies. Describing a person. **Grammar**. Present perfect. **Vocabulary**. Sports and games; word partners; do, play, go; pronunciation, word stress.	**Module 5.** **NCE. Success.** Period (Day) Text Workbook Time 1. Pages 48& 49 36&37 2h 2. Pages 50 & 51 38&39 2h 3. Pages 52 & 53 40&41 2h 4. Pages 54 & 55 42&43 2h 5. Pages 56 & 57 --- 2h Consolidation: pp58 & 59 **IELTS. A Sporting Chance.** Period (Day) Text Workbook Time 1. Pages 50 & 51 23 1.5h 2. Pages 52 & 53 1.5h 3. Pages 54 & 55 24 1.5h 4. Pages 56 & 57 1.5h 5. Pages 58 & 59 25 1.5h This week will not follow the outline exactly, because somewhere in this week there needs to be testing. **Progressive testing week.**	Practice: **Maybe, possibly, probably, if, what if, why, why not.** Choose the best candidate. Preparation. Reading. Task. Speaking Writing: A covering letter Real Life. A formal telephone call. Pronunciation: sounding polite. Improving your spoken fluency. Irregular verbs: p155 Key Language Bank. IELTS. Page 140. * 5. English vocabulary in use. P15 & 16 * 8. English grammar in use. P10 & 11

Week	Function or Skill	Activities	Notes

		Module 6.	Review a
6		**NCE. In the media.**	book/concert/CD.
	Language focus.	Period	Preparation; listening
	-ed/-ing adjectives.	(Day) Text Workbook Time	Task; speaking
	The passive.	1. Pages 60& 61 44&45 2h	Writing a consumer
	Vocabulary.	2. Pages 62 & 63 46&47 2h	review.
	Extreme adjectives.	3. Pages 64 & 65 48&49 2h	English outside the
	Pronunciation: Word stress.	4. Pages 66 & 67 50 -- 2h	classroom.
	Reading and Listening.	5. Pages 68 & 69 --- 2h	
	Listening and vocabulary; TV		Key Language Bank.
	and radio.		IELTS. Page 140.
	Reading and vocabulary; News		
	stories.		
		IELTS. Animal rights and wrongs.	
	Listening.	Period	
	Wildlife film festival.	(Day) Text Workbook Time	
	Note completion.	1. Pages 60 & 61 26 1.5h	Reading the News Paper.
	The right to roam.	2. Pages 62 & 63 1.5h	
	Sentence completion, table	3. Pages 64 & 65 27 1.5h	
	completion.	4. Pages 66 & 67 28 1.5h	
	Speaking.	5. Pages 68 & 69 29 1.5h	
	Discussing animals.		
	Discussing moral issues.	Review: pp70 & 71	
	Writing.		* 5. English vocabulary in
	Presenting and justifying an		use. P17 & 18
	opinion.		* 8. English grammar in
	Analysing the question;		use. P12 & 13
	planning the answer.		
	Grammar.		
	Review of present tenses.		
	Comparison.		
	Vocabulary.		
	Prepositions; word families;		Key Language Bank.
	right word/wrong word.		IELTS. Page 140.

Week	Function or Skill	Activities	Notes

7	Language focus.
	Polite requests.
	Pronunciation; sounding polite
	will for offers and instant
	decisions.
	Pronunciation; 'll
	
	Vocabulary.
	Vocabulary and Speaking;
	Social behaviour.
	Wordspot; *go.*
	Reading and Listening.
	Reading and vocabulary.
	The great international night
	out.
	Listening; social customs in
	Thailand.
	
	Reading.
	Changing lives. Sentence
	completion; matching;
	labelling a diagram.
	The price is wrong.
	Locating information;
	matching multiple choice.
	Speaking.
	Describing places (2)
	Grammar.
	Passive.
	Vocabulary.
	Environment; word families;
	pronunciation; sounds.
		Module 7.
		NCE. Socialising.
		Period
		(Day) Text Workbook Time
		  1. Pages 70& 71 51&52 2h
		  2. Pages 72 & 73 53&54 2h
		  3. Pages 74 & 75 55&56 2h
		  4. Pages 76 & 77 57 -- 2h
		  5. Pages 78 & 79 58 -- 2h
		
		IELTS. Appropriate technology.
		Period
		(Day) Text Workbook Time
		  1. Pages 72 & 73 32 1.5h
		  2. Pages 74 & 75 1.5h
		  3. Pages 76 & 77 33 1.5h
		  4. Pages 78 & 79 --- 1.5h
		  5. Pages 80 & 81 34 1.5h
			Body language
			Black Books
			
			Task; give tips on how to
			behave.
			Preparation; listening
			Task; speaking
			
			Real life; making a social
			arrangement.
			
			* 5. English vocabulary in
			use. P19 & 20
			* 8. English grammar in
			use. P14 & 15
			
			Key Language Bank.
			IELTS. Page 140.

Week	Function or Skill	Activities	Notes
8	Language focus Defining relative clauses Quantifiers Vocabulary How machines work Pronunciation; stress in compound nouns Describing everyday objects Reading and Listening Reading: Machines behaving badly. **Listening**. Mobile phone safety. Multiple choice; note completion Txt don't talk Multiple choice **Speaking**. Discussing communications Internet activities **Writing**. Describing a diagram Selecting information; describing data; introducing a report Presenting and justifying an opinion. **Grammar**. Modal verbs for expressing permission, prohibition and obligation Numerical comparisons **Vocabulary**. Computer terms	**Module 8.** **NCE. Things you can't live without.** Period (Day) Text Workbook Time 1. Pages 80& 81 59&60 2h 2. Pages 82 & 83 61&62 2h 3. Pages 84 & 85 63&64 2h 4. Pages 86 & 87 65 -- 2h 5. Pages 88 & 89 66 -- 2h Consolidation. Pages 90 and 91 **IELTS. Communications.** Period (Day) Text Workbook Time 1. Pages 82 & 83 36 1.5h 2. Pages 84 & 85 1.5h 3. Pages 86 & 87 37 1.5h 4. Pages 88 & 89 --- 1.5h 5. Pages 90 & 91 38 1.5h Academic word study and Review. Pages 92 and 93	Task; make a list of things you'd hate to be without. Preparation; listening Task; speaking Real Life; buying things Writing; saying thank you Irregular verbs: p155 * 5. English vocabulary in use. P20 & 21 * 8. English grammar in use. P15 & 16 Key Language Bank. IELTS. Page 140.

Week	Function or Skill	Activities	Notes
9	Language focus. Making predictions Hypothetical possibilities with *if* Pronunciation: 'll or 'd Vocabulary Society and change. Pronunciation: Shifting stress Wordspot; make Reading and Listening. Reading and vocabulary Getting it right! Getting it wrong!	**Module 9**. **NCE. Future society**. Period (Day) Text Workbook Time 1. Pages 92 & 93 67&68 2h 2. Pages 94 & 95 69&70 2h 3. Pages 96 & 97 71&72 2h 4. Pages 98 & 99 73 -- 2h 5. Pages 100 & 101 74 -- 2h	Task; decide how to spend lottery money Preparation; listening Task; speaking Real life; Ways of saying numbers.
	Reading. Stop the smog Sentence completion; summary completion; How children saved the river. Multiple choice. **Speaking**. How green are you? Expressing degrees of agreement. **Grammar**. Cause and effect -ing v infinitive **Vocabulary**. Word partners; word families; nouns with general meaning.	**IELTS. Earth Matters**. Period (Day) Text Workbook Time 1. Pages 94 & 95 40 1.5h 2. Pages 96 & 97 1.5h 3. Pages 98 & 99 41 1.5h 4. Pages 100 & 101 --- 1.5h 5. Pages 102 & 103 42 1.5h	* 5. English vocabulary in use. P22 & 23 * 8. English grammar in use. P17 & 18 Key Language Bank. IELTS. Page 140.

Week	Function or Skill	Activities	Notes
10	Language focus. Past perfect Pronunciation; Past simple or Past perfect Reported speech Vocabulary Vocabulary and speaking; types of story Wordspot; *say* and *tell* Adverbs for telling stories Reading and vocabulary: the perfect crimes … well almost! Pronunciation; sentence stress **Listening**. Countdown to a healthier life Table completion Milestones of medicine Multiple choice; note completion **Speaking**. Facts about smoking Discussing medical developments **Vocabulary**. Health care and medicine; propositions; register **Writing**. Presenting the solution to a problem Improving your style Describing data Reading the diagram; selecting key information	**Module 10.** **NCE. An Amazing Story.** Period (Day) Text Workbook Time 1. Pages 102& 103 75&76 2h 2. Pages 104 & 105 77&78 2h 3. Pages 106 & 107 79&80 2h 4. Pages 108 & 109 81 -- 2h 5. Pages 110 & 111 82 -- 2h **IELTS. Health check**. Period (Day) Text Workbook Time 1. Pages 104 & 105 44 1.5h 2. Pages 106 & 107 1.5h 3. Pages 108 & 109 44 1.5h 4. Pages 110 & 111 --- 1.5h 5. Pages 112 & 113 46 1.5h Academic word study and Review. Pages 114 and 115 This week will not follow the outline exactly, because somewhere in this week there needs to be testing. **Progressive testing week.**	Task: Tell a ghost story Preparation; speaking Task; speaking and listening. Writing: a narrative Irregular verbs. P155 * Language Summary. Pages 144 - 155 * 5. English vocabulary in use. P24 & 25 * 8. English grammar in use. P19 & 20 **Grammar**. Quantifiers Comparing and contrasting Key Language Bank. IELTS. Page 140.

Week	Function or Skill	Activities	Notes
11	Language focus Obligation and permission in the present Pronunciation; modal verbs Obligation and permission in the past Vocabulary. Wordspot; do Reading and Listening Listening: Annoying rules Reading and vocabulary: to sue or not to sue?	**Module 11.** **NCE. Rules and freedom.** Period (Day) Text Workbook Time 1. Pages 112& 113 83&84 2h 2. Pages 114 & 115 85&86 2h 3. Pages 116 & 117 87&88 2h 4. Pages 118 & 119 --- -- 2h 5. Pages 120 & 121 -- -- 2h	Task: Present your opinions. Preparation: vocabulary Task; speaking Writing; linking words Checking your written work. Review.
	Reading. The formula for happiness; short answer questions; summary completion **Speaking**. Discussing future plans Answering difficult questions **Grammar**. Present tenses with future references Articles **Vocabulary**. Opposites; word families; expressions with self-	**IELTS. Science of happiness**. Period (Day) Text Workbook Time 1. Pages 114 & 115 47 1.5h 2. Pages 116 & 117 1.5h 3. Pages 118 & 119 48 1.5h 4. Pages 120 & 121 --- 1.5h 5. Pages 122 & 123 49 1.5h	* 5. English vocabulary in use. P26 & 27 * 8. English grammar in use. P21 & 22 Key Language Bank. IELTS. Page 140.

Week	Function or Skill	Activities	Notes
12	Language focus. Could have, should have, would have Pronunciation: past modal forms Imaginary situations in the past with *if* Vocabulary. Problems and solutions Wordspot; *think* Reading and Listening Song: Out of reach Pronunciation; vowel sounds	**Module 12.** **NCE. Dilemmas.** Period (Day) Text Workbook Time 1. Pages 122& 123 89&90 2h 2. Pages 124 & 125 91&92 2h 3. Pages 126 & 127 93&94 2h 4. Pages 128 & 129 95 -- 2h 5. Pages 130 & 131 -- -- 2h Consolidation modules. Pages 132 - 133	Introduction to the academic word list. Page 138. Task. Find solutions to problems Preparation; reading and vocabulary Task; speaking Follow up; writing Real life; Saying goodbye.
	Listening. Opera house tour Note completion The Itaipu Dam Note completion; multiple choice; labelling a diagram **Speaking.** Discussing buildings Giving supporting examples **Writing.** Describing objects Presenting the solution to a problem **Grammar.** Participle clauses Unreal conditionals **Vocabulary.** Materials and structures; pronunciation; sounds	**IELTS. Buildings and structures.** Period (Day) Text Workbook Time 1. Pages 124 & 125 51 1.5h 2. Pages 126 & 127 1.5h 3. Pages 128 & 129 52 1.5h 4. Pages 130 & 131 --- 1.5h 5. Pages 132 & 133 53 1.5h Academic word study and Review. Pages 136 and 137	* 5. English vocabulary in use. P28 & 29 * 8. English grammar in use. P23 & 24

Week	Function or Skill	Activities	Notes
13		Consolidation week	
14		Review week	
15		**Testing week.**	

Notes:

Resources:

Required Texts

- *"New Cutting Edge. Intermediate"* Sarah Cunningham. Peter Moor. Pearson Longman. (With mini-dictionary, work book, and teachers book. CD)
- *"Focus on IELTS. Foundation"* Sue O'Connell. Pearson Longman.
- *"The Oxford Advanced Learners Dictionary. 7th Edition"* Oxford University Press. Including CD.
- *EAP Now! Preliminary Student's Book*, Kathy Cox, David Hill, Pearson Education Australia, 2007
- *New Edition Academic Writing Course*, R.R. Jordan, Nelson ELT, 1992
-

Strongly Recommended

- *"English Grammar in Use"* Third Edition. Raymond Murphy. Cambridge University Press. (With CD, and answers)
- *"English Vocabulary in Use"* Second Edition. Stuart Redman. Cambridge University Press. (With CD, and answers)

Useful Texts

- *"Oxford Practice Grammar"* New Series Edition. John Eastwood. Oxford University Press. (With CD, and answers)
- *"Just – Listening and Speaking"* Jeremy Harmer. Marshall Cavendish Pty Ltd. (With CD, and answers)
- *"Just – Reading and Writing"* Jeremy Harmer. Marshall Cavendish Pty Ltd. (With CD, and answers)
- *"Practical English Usage"* Third Edition. Michael Swan. Oxford University Press.
- *"Grammatically Correct"* Anne Stilman. Writer's Digest Books.
- …..
- …..
- Other
- "Insight into IELTS" Vanessa Jakeman and Clare McDowell. Cambridge University Press. (With tapes and answers)
- "IELTS Practice Tests.1 & 2" James Milton. Huw Bell. Peter Neville. Express Publishing.

Section Two: EAP

This is the complete modularised English for Academic Purposes component. This should be worked through <u>at the same time</u> as you are studying **Section One**. There are 10 core weeks in both components, and the material is designed to progress you through the abilities at the same time.

In a full program, a student should be able to master English for Academic Purposes to a very high standard in at least the full fifteen weeks of a standard semester.

Module 1 Customs

Module Overview

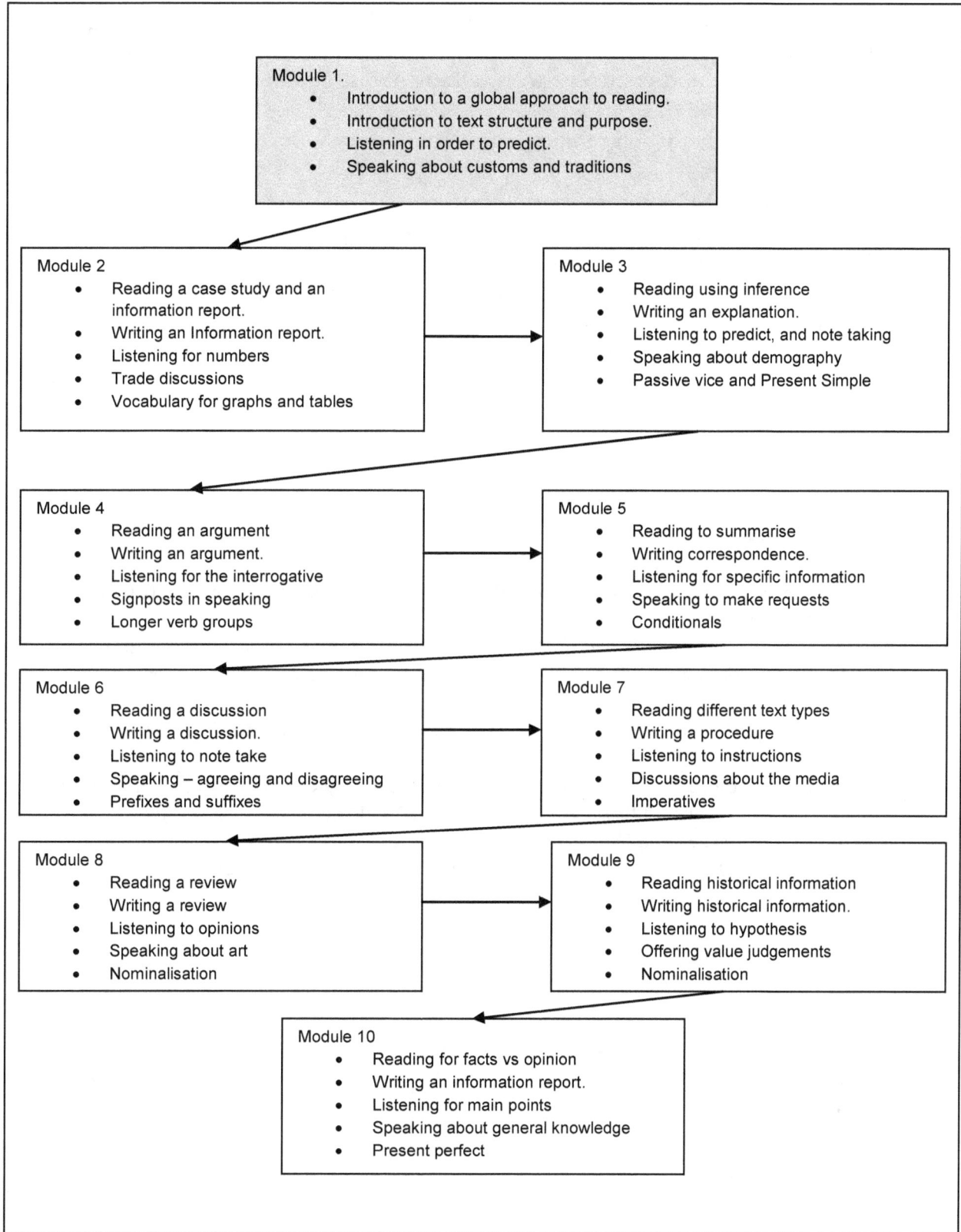

Module 1.
- Introduction to a global approach to reading.
- Introduction to text structure and purpose.
- Listening in order to predict.
- Speaking about customs and traditions

Module 2
- Reading a case study and an information report.
- Writing an Information report.
- Listening for numbers
- Trade discussions
- Vocabulary for graphs and tables

Module 3
- Reading using inference
- Writing an explanation.
- Listening to predict, and note taking
- Speaking about demography
- Passive vice and Present Simple

Module 4
- Reading an argument
- Writing an argument.
- Listening for the interrogative
- Signposts in speaking
- Longer verb groups

Module 5
- Reading to summarise
- Writing correspondence.
- Listening for specific information
- Speaking to make requests
- Conditionals

Module 6
- Reading a discussion
- Writing a discussion.
- Listening to note take
- Speaking – agreeing and disagreeing
- Prefixes and suffixes

Module 7
- Reading different text types
- Writing a procedure
- Listening to instructions
- Discussions about the media
- Imperatives

Module 8
- Reading a review
- Writing a review
- Listening to opinions
- Speaking about art
- Nominalisation

Module 9
- Reading historical information
- Writing historical information.
- Listening to hypothesis
- Offering value judgements
- Nominalisation

Module 10
- Reading for facts vs opinion
- Writing an information report.
- Listening for main points
- Speaking about general knowledge
- Present perfect

Module Objectives

Following completion of this module, you should be able to:

- ➢ Know more vocabulary for talking about customs, culture, romance and marriage
- ➢ Be more fluent and confident with talking about customs, culture, romance and marriage
- ➢ Be able to predict when reading and listening
- ➢ Be able to skim
- ➢ Be more aware of different writing genres
- ➢ Be able to correct mistakes in sentence structure
- ➢ Have practised writing to follow a particular genre
- ➢ Be aware of the reasons why you don't have to understand every word
- ➢ Be aware of style
- ➢ Be aware of specific grammar points

Learning resources

Selected Readings:

1.1: Kathy Cox. David Hill. (2004) *EAP Now! Preliminary*. Pearson Education Australia
1.2: R.R.Jordan. (2007) *New Edition Academic Writing Course*. Longman
1.3: Karen Blanchard. Christine Root. *Ready to Write More: From Paragraph to Essay*. Longman
1.4: Jack C. Richards, Samuela Eckstut-Didier. (2009) *Strategic Reading 2* Cambridge.
1.5: Helen Solorzano, Laurie Frazier. (2009) *Contemporary Topics 1-2*. Longman
1.6: Steven Gershon (2008*) Present Yourself 2: Viewpoints* Cambridge
1.7: Eric Keller, Sylvia T. Warner (2002) *Conversation Gambits* Cambridge
1.8: Michael J. Wallace. (2004) *Study Skills in English* Cambridge

Introductory comment

This unit introduces some of the concepts of academic English, while following a theme that is particularly relevant to students wanting to study cross-culturally: **Culture and customs**.

Module 1

SKILLS	OBJECTIVES
Integrated Skills	Introduction to prediction, skimming, text purpose, critical reading skills To listening for main ideas and specific information To write to follow a genre To order ideas in writing
Writing	To analyse the characteristics of academic writing To examine the process of research and writing To develop organisational skills in writing To introduce text planning skills To analyse paragraph structure To review simple and complex sentences structures
Reading	To use a mono-lingual dictionary effectively in reading To predict information from text titles To analyse the organisation of information in academic texts and develop the use of this to increase reading speed To practise timed reading
Listening	To predict information from lecture titles To interpret paralinguistic cues in speech To introduce and practise skills for listening effectively To introduce listening and note-taking skills
Speaking	To practise asking for information, repetition and clarification in academic settings (Lectures and tutorials)
Study Skills	To familiarise students with assessment procedures and schedule To practise goal setting and time management strategies To develop learning strategies To practise ways of storing and learning vocabulary

Lesson focus

The most common stereotypes about nationalities are based on generalisation about cultures or nationalities.

accurate, active, ambitious, anxious, bright, calm, clever, cheerful, enjoy life, extroverted, family oriented, friendly, generous, good lovers, good drivers, hardworking, honest, impulsive, lazy, loud, lively, modest, nature lovers, nice, open-minded, organized, polite, precise, punctual, patient, sociable, sport lovers, shy, slow, traditional, touchy, well-qualified

1.1 Reading

Read the following text about hamburger. There are missing parts of sentences. Try to correct them.

A hamburger or burger for short is a sandwich consisting of ground meat, ... **O** ... . Hamburgers are often served with lettuce, bacon, tomato, onion, cheese and ... **O** ... . The hamburger has won widespread popularity   ... **O** ... . The term hamburger originally derives from the German city of Hamburg, ... **O** .... . Hamburger can be ... **O** ... in German. The hamburgers are usually mass-produced in factories and frozen for delivery to the site. Hamburgers in fast food restaurants are usually grilled on a flat-top. Hamburgers are often served as a fast dinner, picnic or party food, ... **O** .... .

Right order: ..., ..., ..., ..., ..., ...

and cooked outdoors on barbecue grills
from where many emigrated to America
placed between two buns.
an adjective describing something or somebody from Hamburg
with mustard, mayonnaise or ketchup.
and is known worldwide in chains such as McDonald's or Burger King

1.2 Speaking

Look at the chart below. Go around the class, ask your classmates and tick in the right columns.

Questions	1		2		3		4		5		6	
	yes	no	yes	no	yes	no	yes	no	yes	no	yes	no
Do you like hamburger?												
Do you know it originally comes from Germany?												
Do you know where the city of Hamburg is?												

Do you often eat Hamburger?												
Can you prepare Hamburger by yourself?												

Discuss results in your class. See how many people have the same answers. Use the speaking banks.

Put into the brain storming icons your first associations to some European nationalities. There are some adjectives offered in the exercise above but you can find more on your own, too.

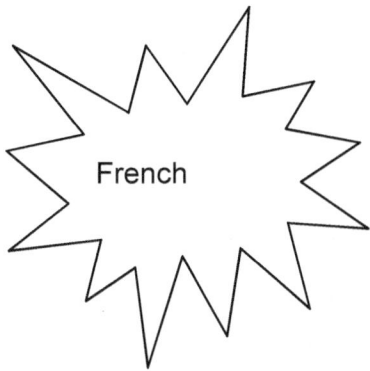

French

Turkish

Englishman/ woman

German

1.3 Writing

Fiction or reality? We had better not to judge before getting to know somebody.
Try to find verbs to the nouns.

	belly dance	*have*
	chess	*dance*
	films subtitled	*do*
	flamenco	*eat*
	languages	*hang*
	nationality food	*learn*
	sockets to the chimney	*listen*
	strange food abroad	*play*
	to music	*talk*
	to tourists	*try*
	a chat in foreign languages	*watch*

What nationality can you associate?

	apple pie	*American*
	beer	*Scottish*
	breakfast	*Irish*
	chocolate	*English*
	coffee	*German*
	competitive sport	*Russian*
	football	*Dutch*
	kit	*Brazilian*
	orange	*Japanese*
	pizza	*Greek*
	restaurant	*Italian*
	salad	*Spanish*
	tricolour	*Swiss*
	tulip	*Chinese*
	vodka	*French*
	wine	*Hungarian*

Where does she or he come from? Write the countries on the line.

Einstein is from	Princess Sissy is from	Bruce Willis is from	Queen Elisabeth II is from ....
Russel Crow is from	Ronaldo is from	Alain Delon is from	Banderas is from ....

What do you mean how you can get know other nationalities? **Sum up your ideas and write some sentences about. To tell your opinion you can use the speaking bank bellow.**

As far as I 'm concerned	I don't really know (if)/ I don't think
As I see it,	I think (that) …
From my point of view	In my view / opinion …
I am convinced (that)	Personnaly, I think …
I am not sure (about / if)	To my mind, …

Closure

Stereotypes are based on appearance, language, food, habits, psychological traits, attitudes, values of other nationalities. But in the focus there should stay tolerance. **As closure the lesson 'Stereotypes in multicultural Europe', play in teams and identify Europaen countries. Who can find the most in 3 minutes?**

© kisss

Right order: 3, 5, 6, 2, 4, 1

Link to text Hamburger http://en.wikipedia.org/wiki/Hamburger

do	belly dance
play	chess
watch	films subtitled
dance	flamenco
learn	languages
eat	nationality food
hang	sockets to the chimney
cook	strange food abroad
listen	to music
talk	to tourists
have	a chat in foreign languages

American	apple pie
German	beer
English	breakfast
Swiss	chocolate
Irish	coffee
Japanese	competitive sport
Brazilian	football
Scottish	kilt
Spanish	orange
Italian	pizza
Chinese	restaurant
Greek	salad
French	tricolours
Dutch	tulip
Russian	vodka
Hungarian	wine

Einstein is from *Germany*.	Princess Sissy is from *Austria*.	Bruce Willis is from *the USA*.	Queen Elisabeth II is from *England*.
Russel Crow is from *Australia*.	Ronaldo is from *Portugal*.	Alain Delon is from *France*.	Banderas is from *Spain*.

Reading activity

Selected reading

Unit 1. EAP Now! Preliminary. Kathy Cox & David Hill. 2007.

References

CEFR Levels http://www.coe.int/T/DG4/Portfolio/?L=E&M=/main_pages/levels.html

Guidelines on Intercultural Education (UNESCO 2006)
http://unesdoc.unesco.org/images/0014/001478/147878e.pdf

Intercultural education in the primary school (NCCA 2005)
http://www.ncca.ie/uploadedfiles/publications/intercultural.pdf

Module 2 Trade

Module Overview

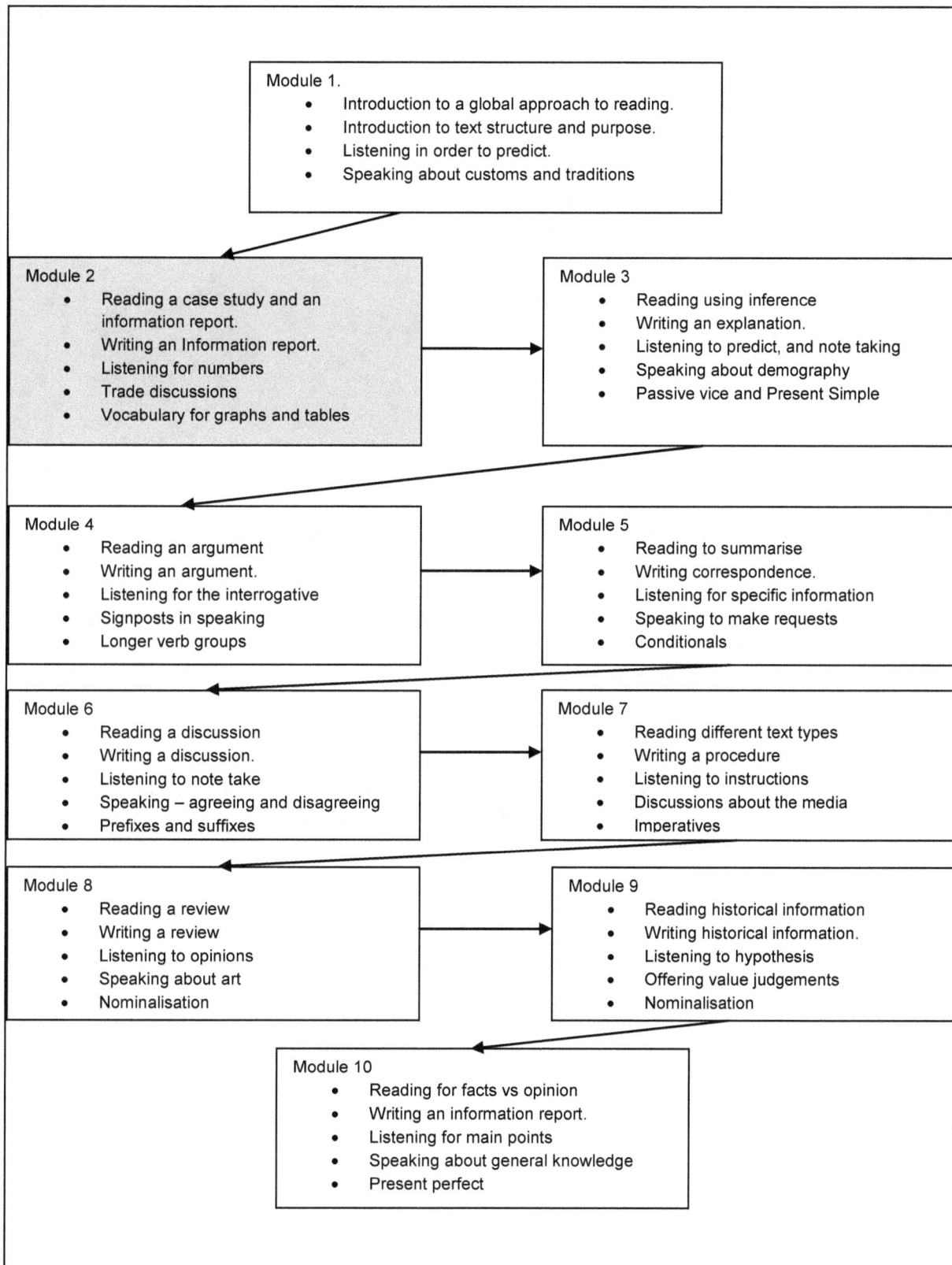

Module 1.
- Introduction to a global approach to reading.
- Introduction to text structure and purpose.
- Listening in order to predict.
- Speaking about customs and traditions

Module 2
- Reading a case study and an information report.
- Writing an Information report.
- Listening for numbers
- Trade discussions
- Vocabulary for graphs and tables

Module 3
- Reading using inference
- Writing an explanation.
- Listening to predict, and note taking
- Speaking about demography
- Passive vice and Present Simple

Module 4
- Reading an argument
- Writing an argument.
- Listening for the interrogative
- Signposts in speaking
- Longer verb groups

Module 5
- Reading to summarise
- Writing correspondence.
- Listening for specific information
- Speaking to make requests
- Conditionals

Module 6
- Reading a discussion
- Writing a discussion.
- Listening to note take
- Speaking – agreeing and disagreeing
- Prefixes and suffixes

Module 7
- Reading different text types
- Writing a procedure
- Listening to instructions
- Discussions about the media
- Imperatives

Module 8
- Reading a review
- Writing a review
- Listening to opinions
- Speaking about art
- Nominalisation

Module 9
- Reading historical information
- Writing historical information.
- Listening to hypothesis
- Offering value judgements
- Nominalisation

Module 10
- Reading for facts vs opinion
- Writing an information report.
- Listening for main points
- Speaking about general knowledge
- Present perfect

Module Objectives

Following completion of this module, you should be able to:

- ➢ Know more vocabulary about trade
- ➢ Recognise and understand a case study
- ➢ Be able to make generalisations in English
- ➢ Be able to scan a text to locate specific information
- ➢ Know more nouns and verbs for describing things
- ➢ Be able to describe graphs and tables
- ➢ Be able to write an information report
- ➢ Have practised ways of expressing the past
- ➢ Have practised ways of giving opinions

Learning resources

Selected Readings:

1.1: Kathy Cox. David Hill. (2004) *EAP Now! Preliminary*. Pearson Education Australia
1.2: R.R.Jordan. (2007) *New Edition Academic Writing Course*. Longman
1.3: Karen Blanchard. Christine Root. *Ready to Write More: From Paragraph to Essay*. Longman
1.4: Jack C. Richards, Samuela Eckstut-Didier. (2009) *Strategic Reading 2* Cambridge.
1.5: Helen Solorzano, Laurie Frazier. (2009) *Contemporary Topics 1-2*. Longman
1.6: Steven Gershon (2008*) Present Yourself 2: Viewpoints* Cambridge
1.7: Eric Keller, Sylvia T. Warner (2002) *Conversation Gambits* Cambridge
1.8: Michael J. Wallace. (2004) *Study Skills in English* Cambridge

Introductory comment

This unit introduces some of the concepts of written academic English, while following a theme that is particularly relevant to students wanting to study cross-culturally: **Trade**.

Module 2

SKILLS	OBJECTIVES
Integrated Skills	To make generalisations To give spoken explanation signalling new stages To scan and find meaning from context To describe graphs and tables To write an information report
Writing	To practise writing introductory and concluding paragraphs To practise writing paraphrases To practise writing summaries To develop organisational skills in writing - sequence markers
Reading	To use a mono-lingual dictionary effectively in reading To predict information from text titles To analyse the organisation of information in academic texts and develop the use of this to increase reading speed To practise timed reading
Listening	To predict information from lecture titles To interpret paralinguistic cues in speech To introduce and practise skills for listening effectively To introduce listening and note-taking skills
Speaking	To analyse and practise various elements of speaking in public (volume, speed, articulation)
Study Skills	Students advise teacher of area of study for Assessment 1: Report First draft due week 4, final due week 5

2.1 Trade: Core Vocabulary

These core vocabulary reference sheets provide between 150 and 240 key words and phrases for each industry. Each series is divided into three pages that, when combined, form an alphabetical list. In taking this lexical approach to attaining key vocabulary, students should be encouraged to translate the specific words and phrases into their native tongues as each phrase has a very specific translation in each language.

antislip
assemble-to-order product
to assemble
assembly - assembly process
assembly line
automation
auxiliary materials
backlog
bar chart
bar code
batch
breaking load
bulk production
by-product
colleague
computer-designed
computer-integrated
manufacturing
consumption per unit
continuous processing line
custom-made goods
defect
to design
designer
direct cost
direct product profitability
distribution expenses
to draw a plan
dynamometer - tensile-strength
tester
electrostatic charge
endurance test
energy costs
equipment
equipment purchase
factory
factory overheads - industrial
overheads
to pack - to wrap
pack
packaging room
packing - packaging
packing department
personnel management
personnel rotation
personnel turnover - personnel
replacement
piece-work
piece - item
pilot plant
plant manager
price tag
processing method
produce - to manufacture

producer - manufacturer
product analysis
product design
product mix
product range
product specialization
production - output
production constraints
production cost
production cycle
production factors
production index
production management
production manager
production methods
production overheads
production planning
production potential
production prices
production process faulty - flawed
feasibility
final inspection
finished goods inventory
finished product
fixed manufacturing costs
floor manager - department
manager
flow production
flowchart
goods lift (GB) - goods elevator
(US)
hanging tag
in process of completion
in progress
in stock
industrial area
industrial espionage
industrial plant
industrial processes
industrial production
industrial property
inflammable
to innovate
innovation
innovative
input
invest in equipment
job order
know-how
to label
label
laboratory
laboratory test
labour cost per output unit

labour hand-work - manual labour
large scale production
production progress
production standards
production statement
production time - manufacturing
time
production volume ratio
production worker
productive
productive capacity
productivity
productivity indicators
programme - to schedule
progress control
project
project management
project manager
project planning
prototype
quality certificate
quality circle (QC)
quality control
quality criteria
quality of output ratio
randomized sample
raw material
research and development (R&D)
research laboratory
safety device
safety measures
safety stock - safety inventory
scatter chart
semi-finished goods
semi-finished product
sequencing
shortage of raw materials
spare part
learning curve
line worker
logistics
machine-hours
to machine
machine loading
machine tools
machinery and equipment
main product
maintenance
Maintenance and Repair Handling
(MRH)
to make to order - to make on
request
manometer - pressure gauge
manufacturer's brand

manufacturing
manufacturing cost
manufacturing expenses
manufacturing industry
manufacturing overheads
manufacturing plants
to mass-produce
mass production
notice board
off-the-shelf
one-off production
operations scheduling
optical scanner - reader
to order
order backlog
out of order
output
output of a plant
overcapacity
overhead costs - overheads
to overproduce
overproduction
specific-purpose equipment
sticker
stock (GB) - inventory (US)
stock card - inventory listing
stock depletion
stock level
stock turnover - inventory
turnover
storage costs
to store - to stock
store - warehouse
substandard
supplier
tag
technical consultant
technical sheet
technological gap
tensiometer
to test
tester
throughputs
timing - time scheduling
total output
toxic
twist counter
to unpack
unsold stocks - leftover stocks
warehouse - stockroom
warehouseman - storekeeper
to waste
waste goods
work-in-process products
work order cost
working conditions
workstation
zero-defect purchase

Logistics

a nonstop flight
actual time of departure
advance freight - prepaid freight
advice of shipment - shipping
notice - advice note

agreed airport of departure
agreed tare
air waybill (AWB) - air
consignment note
all-up weight
allowed tolerances
at the border
average survey
backed note
barrel
batch number
bearer bill of lading
below deck
berth - mooring
bill of entry
bill of lading (B/L)
boarding card
bonded warehouse - customs
warehouse
border - frontier
bulk cargo
by mail - by post
cardboard box - carton
cargo - load
cargo insurance
cargo plane - freight plane
carriage - transport (GB) -
transportation (US)
carriage by sea - sea transport
carriage forward
carriage paid
carrier
certificate of origin
certificate of shipment
charter party
CIF value
clearance
clearance agent
clearance certificate
handling costs
harbour dues - harbour fees
harbour office
heavy traffic
hold
home delivery
house air waybill (HAWB)
import duties
import licence
in bond - waiting for clearance
in bulk
in transit
inch
inspection certificate
kilogramme - kilo
landed terms
landing
landing card
landing order - discharging permit

litre (GB) - liter (US)
loading and unloading charges
loading area
loading unit
lorry (GB) - truck (US)
lot
luggage (GB) - baggage (US)
metre (GB) - meter (US)
mile
millimetre
moorage
net tonnage
net weight
on arrival
on board
on deck
ounce
outward journey
overland forwarding
overload
owner's risk rate
clearance documents
clearance duty
cleared - ex bond - duty paid
collection of goods
consignee
consignor's name
consignor
consular invoice
container
container terminal
containership
cost and freight (C&F)
cost, insurance and freight (CIF)
cubic
cubic volume - cubic capacity
custom-house - customs
customs declaration form
customs formalities
customs guard - customs officer
customs invoice
customs officer
customs rate
customs regulations
declared value
delivered at frontier (DAF)
delivered duty paid (DDP)
delivery ex warehouse
delivery notice
delivery weight
destination
dock - quay - wharf
docker (GB) - longshoreman (US)
documents against acceptance
documents against payment
driver
duty-free
duty

duty paid
duty unpaid
entry visa
packing list
part load
part shipment
payload
place of delivery
place of departure
place of destination
port - harbour (GB) - harbor (US)
port authorities
port of arrival
port of call
port of departure
port of destination
port of discharge - port of delivery
porterage
postage
poste restante (GB) - general delivery (US)
pound
preferential rate
preliminary inspection
product loss during loading
protective duty
rail shipment - rail forwarding
reply paid
right of way
road transport - haulage
rummaging
scheduled time of arrival
scheduled time of departure
sender's name
sender
ship - vessel
shipment
shipowner company
shipping agent
shipping company
shipping cubage
shipping documents
shipping instructions
shipping note (S/N)
to charter a ship
to clear the goods
dock
ex factory - ex works
ex ship
ex warehouse
excess luggage (GB) - excess baggage (US)
export permit
failure - damage
flat-rate
foot
forwarder's receipt
forwarding agent
forwarding station
free-trade area
free carrier
free delivered
free delivery
free in and out (FIO)
free of all average

free of charges
free on board (FOB)
free on board airport
free on quay (FOQ) - free at wharf
free on truck
free port
freepost
freight - freightage
freight charges
freight payable at destination
freight prepaid
freight rate
from port to port
full container load (FCL)
goods handling
goods train (GB) - freight train (US)
goods wagon (GB) - freight car (US)
goods yard (GB) - freight yard (US)
gram - gramme
gross
gross weight
hand luggage
to handle with care
high seas
land
to rent a car
to send goods - to ship goods
to ship
single ticket (GB) - one-way ticket (US)
specified port - agreed port
storage - warehousing
storage costs - warehousing costs
to store
to stow
stowage charges
subject to duty
tare - tare weight
terms of delivery
time zone difference
tolerance
toll-free
ton
tonnage
trailer
tranship
transhipment - transloading
transport by rail
transport plane
unit of measurement
unloading operations
unpacked
warehouse receipt
warehousing - storage
waybill - consignment note
weigh
weighing
weight
weight limit
weight specified in the invoice
yard

INTERNATIONAL (TRADE) ORGANIZATIONS

UN	IMF	EU	ICC
ITO	NATO	OEEC	OPEC
APEC	GATT	WTO	OECD

The .... was the outcome of the failure of negotiating governments to create the International Trade Organization (ITO). It was formed in 1947 and lasted until 1994, when it was replaced by the World Trade Organization in 1995. The Bretton Woods Conference had introduced the idea for an organization to regulate trade as part of a larger plan for economic recovery after World War II. As governments negotiated the ITO, 15 negotiating states began parallel negotiations for the .... as a way to attain early tariff reductions. Once the ITO failed in 1950, only the .... agreement was left. Its main objective was the reduction of barriers to international trade. This was achieved through the reduction of tariff barriers, quantitative restrictions and subsidies on trade through a series of agreements.

The Bretton Woods Conference of 1944 recognized the need for a comparable international institution for trade (the later proposed ....) to complement the International Monetary Fund and the World Bank. Probably because Bretton Woods was attended only by representatives of finance ministries and not by representatives of trade ministries, an agreement covering trade was not negotiated there. At the proposal of the United States, the UNESC adopted a resolution, in February 1946, calling for a conference to draft a charter for a(n).................................. March 1948, the negotiations on the .... Charter were successfully completed in Havana. The Charter provided for the establishment of the ...., and set out the basic rules for international trade and other international economic matters. The Charter, however, never entered into force; while repeatedly submitted to the US Congress, it was never approved.

The .... is an international organization designed by its founders to supervise and liberalize international capital trade. The organization officially commenced on January 1, 1995 under the Marrakesh Agreement, replacing the General Agreement on Tariffs and Trade (GATT), which commenced in 1947. It deals with regulation of trade between participating countries; it provides a framework for negotiating and formalising trade agreements, and a dispute resolution process aimed at enforcing participants' adherence to ....agreements which are signed by representatives of member governments and ratified by their parliaments.

The ....is the largest, most representative business organization in the world. Its hundreds of thousands of member companies in over 130 countries have interests spanning every sector of private enterprise.A world network of national committees keeps the .... International Secretariat in Paris informed about national and regional business priorities. More than 2,000 experts drawn from its member companies feed their knowledge and experience into crafting the .... stance on specific business issues. The United Nations, the World Trade Organization, and many other intergovernmental bodies, both international and regional, are kept in touch with the views of international business through it.

.... is a forum for 21 Pacific Rim countries (styled 'member economies') to cooperate on regional trade and investment liberalisation and facilitation. Its objective is to enhance economic growth and prosperity in the region and to strengthen the Asia-Pacific community. Members account for approximately 40% of the world's population, approximately 54% of world GDP and about 44% of world trade.

The .... is an international organization whose stated aims are facilitating cooperation in international law, international security, economic development, social progress, human rights, and the achieving of world peace. It was founded in 1945 after World War II to replace the League of Nations, to stop wars between countries, and to provide a platform for dialogue. It contains multiple subsidiary organizations to carry out its missions.

The .... is an intergovernmental military alliance based on a treaty which was signed on April 4, 1949. Its headquarters are in Brussels, Belgium, and the organization constitutes a system of collective defense whereby its member states agree to mutual defense in response to an attack by any external party.

The .... is an economic and political union of 27 member states. Committed to regional integration, it was established by the Treaty of Maastricht on 1 November 1993 upon the foundations of the pre-existing EEC. With almost 500 million citizens, it combined generates an estimated 30% share (US$18.4 trillion in 2008) of the nominal gross world product.

The .... is an international organization that oversees the global financial system by following the macroeconomic policies of its member countries, in particular those with an impact on exchange rates and the balance of payments. It is an organization formed with a stated objective of stabilizing international exchange rates and facilitating development. It also offers highly leveraged loans mainly to poorer countries. Its headquarters are located in Washington, D.C., United States.

The .... is an international organisation of 30 countries that accept the principles of representative democracy and free-market economy. Most of its members are high-income economies with a high HDI and are regarded as developed countries.

The .... was founded in 1948 to help the <u>Marshall Plan</u> for the reconstruction of <u>Europe</u> after <u>World War II</u>. The headquarters was in the Chateau de la Muette in Paris, France. As the Marshall Plan was out of date , it focused on economic questions

The .... is a <u>cartel</u> of twelve countries made up of <u>Algeria</u>, <u>Angola</u>, <u>Ecuador</u>, <u>Iran</u>, <u>Iraq</u>, <u>Kuwait</u>, <u>Libya</u>, <u>Nigeria</u>, <u>Qatar</u>, <u>Saudi Arabia</u>, the <u>United Arab Emirates</u>, and <u>Venezuela</u>. OPEC has maintained its headquarters in <u>Vienna</u> since 1965, and hosts regular meetings among the oil ministers of its Member Countries. <u>Indonesia</u> withdrew its membership in 2008 after it became a net importer of oil, but stated it would likely return if it became a net exporter in the world again.

What do these abbreviations stand for?

UN	IMF	EU
ICC	ITO	NATO
OEEC	OPEC	APEC
GATT	WTO	OECD
UNESC	EEC	HDI

PRESENT PERFECT

We use the present perfect to talk about something that happened in the past at an unspecified time.

We form the present perfect with the auxiliary verb **has/have + the past participle of the main verb.**

Example: **I have just eaten a sandwich**.

TIME MARKERS

Just: We use **just** in affirmative sentences.

Already: We use **already** in affirmative sentences.

Yet: We use **yet** in negative sentences and in questions.

Ever: We use **ever** in questions.

Never: We use **never** in affirmative sentences.

For and Since: We use for and since to talk about something that started in the past and continues in the present.

For+Period of time: For a week, for two hours, for three hours.

Since+The point in time when it started: Since March, since 2009

Complete the chart

Infinitive	Past Simple	Past Participle
be	was-were	
buy		bought
cut	cut	
drink	drank	
eat		eaten
go		gone
make	made	
read	read	
run		run
write	wrote	

Complete the Sentences With Ever Or Never

1- Have you _____ eaten sushi?
2- Has she _____ worn skirts?
3- I have _____ done yoga
4- She has_____ played tennis
5- They have _____ drunk tea
6- Has he _____ travelled abroad?
7- They have _____ written a letter
8- He has _____ gone dancing

Complete with already or yet.

1- I'm not hungry. i have .... eaten a sandwich.
2- He hasn't finished his homework............
3- a: Have you sent the e-mail ....?
   b: Yes, I have .... sent it.
4- They haven't had a test..........
5- I have .... seen this film.
6- They have .... phoned his friends
7- Have you bought the milk ....?

Complete the sentences with for or since.

1- He has had his job...........2001.
2- I haven't seen paul .... ages
3- He has waited for the bus ....15 minutes
4- They haven't visited their parents .... March
5- I haven't eaten ....midday
6- She has been ill .... tuesday
7- They haven't met their friends .... holidays

Complete the sentences with the right form of the verb in brackets.

1- He _____(just read) the letter.
2- They _____ (not meet) sally yet.
3- The teacher _____ (give) us a lot of homework.
4- _____you_____ (buy) her a present for her birthday?
5- He _____ (not invite) her to the party yet.
6- _____ he_____ (write) the letters yet?
7- My friend _____(just phone) from paris
8- They _____(already/have breakfast).

Write sentences in affirmative (a) negative (n) and interrogative (?) form.

1- You / make / a cake (?)
2- We / see this film (a)
3- He / pass / his driving test (n)
4- She / lose / her keys (a)
5- You / see / my books (?)
6- I / break / the new vase (a)
7- The dog / eat / all the food (n)

Complete the sentences with the correct verb from the box.

study   give   buy   spend

understand   paint   made   swim

1- She has just.............. a lot of sandwiches.
2- They have .... the walls yellow.
3- Has she............. the lesson?
4- You haven't .... geography for today.
5- She has .... all her money on clothes.
6- They haven't .... in the pool yet.
7- My mother has .... a cake for my birthday
8- My father has .... me a car after passing my driving test

Choose the right option.

1. I haven't watched a film since / for January.
2- She haven't/ hasn't bought a new dress for the party.
3- They have already / yet swum in the sea.
4- Has /have she invited all her friends to the party?
5- He has drank/ drunk all the coffee.
6- I haven't watered the plants already/ yet.
7- She has taught the same subject since / for ten years.

Key references for further study

Reading activity

Selected reading

Unit 2. EAP Now! Preliminary. Kathy Cox & David Hill. 2007.

References

Module 3 Demography

Module Overview

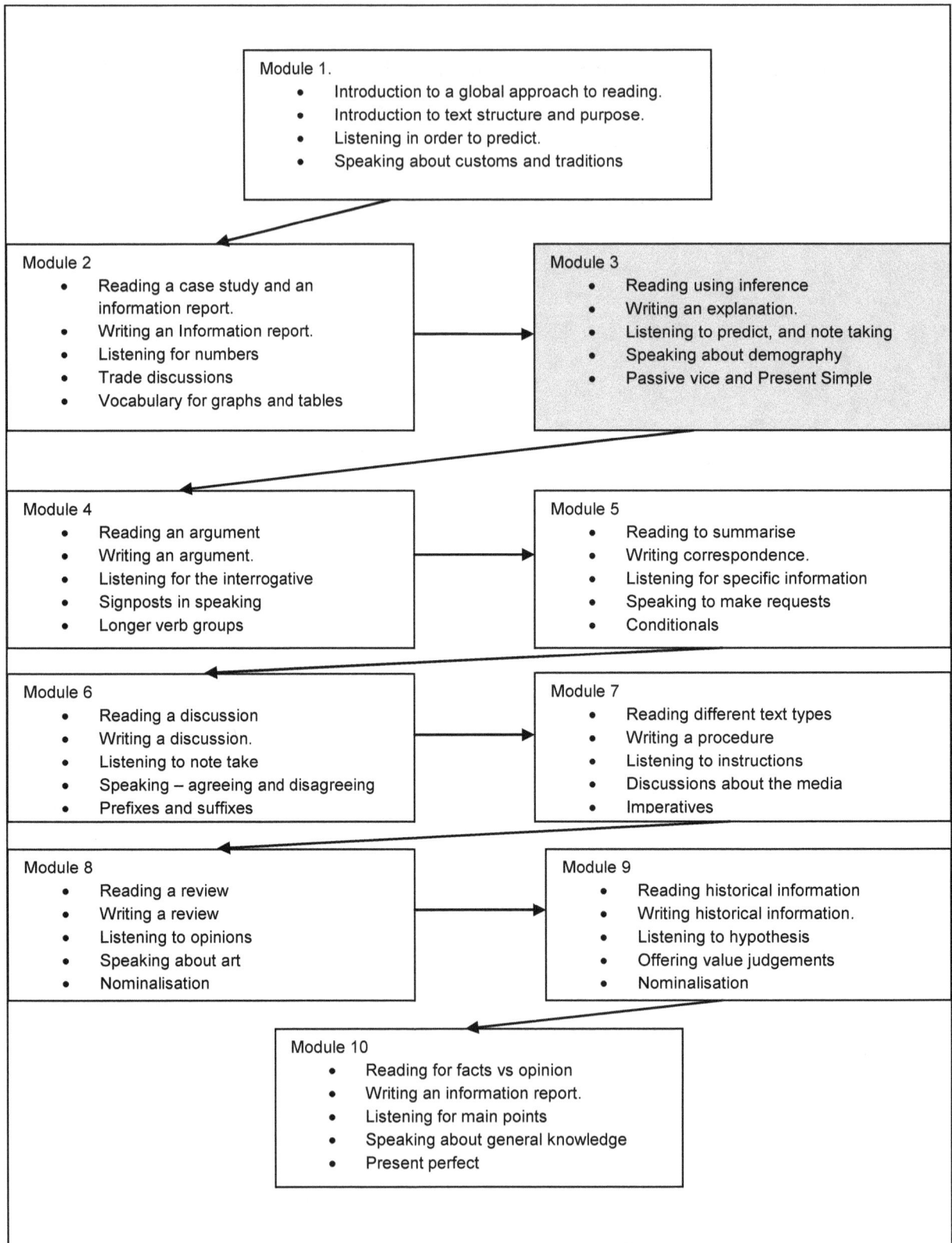

Module 1.
- Introduction to a global approach to reading.
- Introduction to text structure and purpose.
- Listening in order to predict.
- Speaking about customs and traditions

Module 2
- Reading a case study and an information report.
- Writing an Information report.
- Listening for numbers
- Trade discussions
- Vocabulary for graphs and tables

Module 3
- Reading using inference
- Writing an explanation.
- Listening to predict, and note taking
- Speaking about demography
- Passive vice and Present Simple

Module 4
- Reading an argument
- Writing an argument.
- Listening for the interrogative
- Signposts in speaking
- Longer verb groups

Module 5
- Reading to summarise
- Writing correspondence.
- Listening for specific information
- Speaking to make requests
- Conditionals

Module 6
- Reading a discussion
- Writing a discussion.
- Listening to note take
- Speaking – agreeing and disagreeing
- Prefixes and suffixes

Module 7
- Reading different text types
- Writing a procedure
- Listening to instructions
- Discussions about the media
- Imperatives

Module 8
- Reading a review
- Writing a review
- Listening to opinions
- Speaking about art
- Nominalisation

Module 9
- Reading historical information
- Writing historical information.
- Listening to hypothesis
- Offering value judgements
- Nominalisation

Module 10
- Reading for facts vs opinion
- Writing an information report.
- Listening for main points
- Speaking about general knowledge
- Present perfect

Module Objectives

Following completion of this module, you should be able to:

- ➤ Know more vocabulary for talking about societies and people
- ➤ Be more fluent and confident with talking about societies and people
- ➤ Have improved ability to predict the content of an article from the introduction
- ➤ Be able to pronounce many nouns and verbs with the word stress in the correct place
- ➤ Know the stages to expect when reading an explanation essay
- ➤ Be able to write a short explanation essay with appropriate staging
- ➤ Have experienced listening to people with different accents
- ➤ Be able to recognise and talk about general facts
- ➤ Be able to ask for clarification when something is not understood

Learning resources

Selected Readings:

1.9: Kathy Cox. David Hill. (2004) *EAP Now! Preliminary*. Pearson Education Australia

1.10: R.R.Jordan. (2007) *New Edition Academic Writing Course*. Longman

1.11: Karen Blanchard. Christine Root. *Ready to Write More: From Paragraph to Essay*. Longman

1.12: Jack C. Richards, Samuela Eckstut-Didier. (2009) *Strategic Reading 2* Cambridge.

1.13: Helen Solorzano, Laurie Frazier. (2009) *Contemporary Topics 1-2*. Longman

1.14: Steven Gershon (2008) *Present Yourself 2: Viewpoints* Cambridge

1.15: Eric Keller, Sylvia T. Warner (2002) *Conversation Gambits* Cambridge

1.16: Michael J. Wallace. (2004) *Study Skills in English* Cambridge

Introductory comment

This unit could be called *Social Change* or *Society.* The aim is to lead students into talking in the general ways that are necessary for academic and less-practical vocational courses. The topic allows wide ranging discussion on society as a whole, something that is likely to be of interest to most students, and relevant to the kinds of topics that come up in many international English language examinations: **Demographics**.

Parts of Speech : Common Nouns

Definition: A **common noun** is an idea, person, place, or thing. It can be acted upon and is capitalized only at the start of a sentence. A common noun can be a single word, a group of words, or a hyphenated word.

Examples: It takes *self-control*   idea
for a *teenager*   person
to drive to *school*   place
in a *sports car*.   thing

Writing Hints
Whenever possible, use specific common nouns rather than general common nouns.

Practice
Sort the following common nouns as an idea, person, place, or thing in the correct columns:

mountain, friendship, teacher, neighborhood, food, self-image, freedom, toy, fire-fighter, cousin, rock, country, lamp stand, football stadium, police officer, self-confidence, grandfather clock, family room, brother-in-law, world peace

IDEA	PERSON	PLACE	THING
_____	_____	_____	_____
_____	_____	_____	_____
_____	_____	_____	_____
_____	_____	_____	_____
_____	_____	_____	_____

Application

Compose four sentences, using a common noun from each category. Use none of the common nouns listed on this worksheet. Be as specific as possible.

idea

_____

person

_____

place

_____

thing

_____

Parts of Speech Proper Nouns   **Name**

_____

Definition: A **proper noun** is the name of a person, place, or thing. It can be acted upon and is capitalized. A proper noun may be a single word, a group of words (with or without abbreviations), or a hyphenated word.

Examples: *Josh* was honored   person
        at *U.S. Memorial Auditorium*   place
        with the *Smith-Lee Award*.   thing

Writing Hints

Capitalize all words that make up proper nouns, except articles (*a*, *an*, and *the*), prepositions, such as *of*, *to*, and *from*, and conjunctions, such as *and*, *or*, and *but*.

Practice

Circle the proper nouns in the following story. Make sure to circle all words belonging to each proper noun.

    John Francis left his home in Beatrice, Nebraska in 1941, shortly before the start of World War II. Traveling first by bus to Chicago, he then boarded the *Southwestern Chief* to ride to Los Angeles. At Grand Central Station, John met his sister, Jane, and immediately began looking for part-time work and an apartment. He found employment at Blix Hardware on Western Avenue and a room to rent in nearby South Hollywood.

    When war was declared, John enlisted in the army and was stationed at Fort Ord. He played trumpet in the Army Band and was promoted to the rank of Staff Sergeant. The United States was fortunate to have so many young men, like John, serving their country.

After the war in 1945, John enrolled in the University of Southern California, paying his tuition with money from the G.I. Bill. Graduating Cum Laude with degrees in Business and Social Science, he continued to play trumpet in clubs all over Southern California. Upon marrying Janice Jones, he took a job at California Federal Savings and Loan and was promoted to Senior Vice-President. He and his wife raised two children, who both graduated from the University of California at Los Angeles. John retired in 1980 to travel and play his trumpet.

Application

Compose your own sentence with person, place, and thing proper nouns.

_____

_____

Module 3

SKILLS	OBJECTIVES
Integrated Skills	To predict meaning from context To write an explanation essay To use passive voice To listen and take notes
Writing	To practise analysing assignment tasks To practise planning and writing reports To practise writing descriptions of processes and procedures including describing information presented in non-linear texts
Reading	To practise skimming To practise strategies for dealing with unknown vocabulary To practise identifying the main idea in a text To practise timed reading To practise reading graphs and tables To practise identifying sequence in texts
Listening	To practise listening for main ideas in a text To practise listening for connectives and sequence markers to assist comprehension To practise listening for facts and/or specific information To practise taking notes on the description of a process
Speaking	To review all English sounds and the phonetic alphabet To identify individual difficulties
Study Skills	Report presentation including formatting and title pages

Key references for further study

Reading activity

Selected reading

Unit 3. EAP Now! Preliminary. Kathy Cox & David Hill. 2007.

References

Module 4 Energy

Module Overview

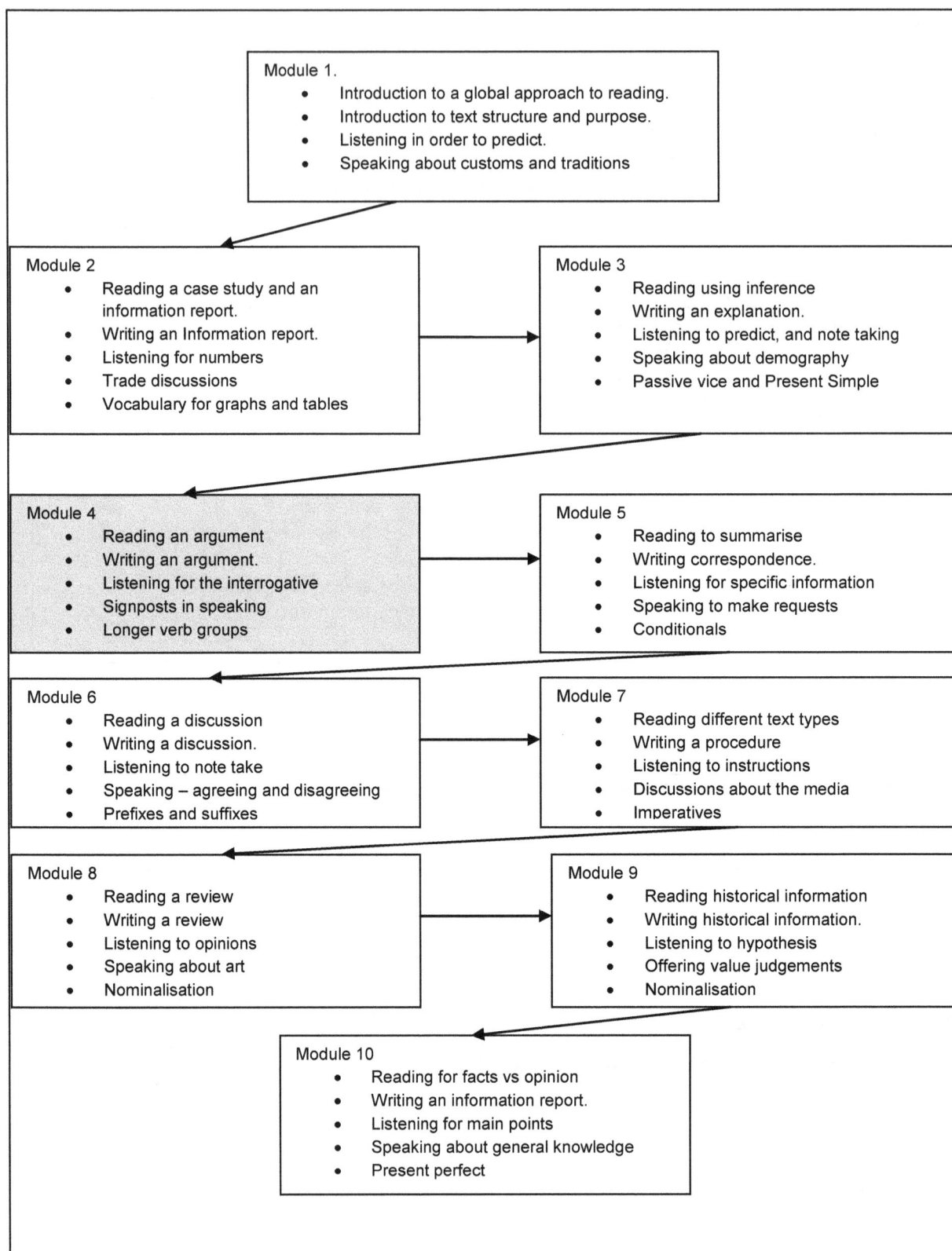

Module 1.
- Introduction to a global approach to reading.
- Introduction to text structure and purpose.
- Listening in order to predict.
- Speaking about customs and traditions

Module 2
- Reading a case study and an information report.
- Writing an Information report.
- Listening for numbers
- Trade discussions
- Vocabulary for graphs and tables

Module 3
- Reading using inference
- Writing an explanation.
- Listening to predict, and note taking
- Speaking about demography
- Passive vice and Present Simple

Module 4
- Reading an argument
- Writing an argument.
- Listening for the interrogative
- Signposts in speaking
- Longer verb groups

Module 5
- Reading to summarise
- Writing correspondence.
- Listening for specific information
- Speaking to make requests
- Conditionals

Module 6
- Reading a discussion
- Writing a discussion.
- Listening to note take
- Speaking – agreeing and disagreeing
- Prefixes and suffixes

Module 7
- Reading different text types
- Writing a procedure
- Listening to instructions
- Discussions about the media
- Imperatives

Module 8
- Reading a review
- Writing a review
- Listening to opinions
- Speaking about art
- Nominalisation

Module 9
- Reading historical information
- Writing historical information.
- Listening to hypothesis
- Offering value judgements
- Nominalisation

Module 10
- Reading for facts vs opinion
- Writing an information report.
- Listening for main points
- Speaking about general knowledge
- Present perfect

Module Objectives

Following completion of this module, you should be able to:

- ➢ Understand and be able to use various meanings of energy
- ➢ Understand *For* and *Against* and have a concept of 'issues'
- ➢ Find definitions in context and the clues or signals that locate those definitions
- ➢ Be able to read a graph and work in the present tense to describe it
- ➢ Locate stages in an argument and write topic sentences
- ➢ Write an argument using staging
- ➢ Have experienced listening to people with different accents
- ➢ Differentiate verb forms and functions in phrases
- ➢ Compose an argument and speak using signposting for the listener

Learning resources

Selected Readings:

1.17: Kathy Cox. David Hill. (2004) *EAP Now! Preliminary*. Pearson Education Australia
1.18: R.R.Jordan. (2007) *New Edition Academic Writing Course*. Longman
1.19: Karen Blanchard. Christine Root. *Ready to Write More: From Paragraph to Essay*. Longman
1.20: Jack C. Richards, Samuela Eckstut-Didier. (2009) *Strategic Reading 2* Cambridge.
1.21: Helen Solorzano, Laurie Frazier. (2009) *Contemporary Topics 1-2*. Longman
1.22: Steven Gershon (2008*) Present Yourself 2: Viewpoints* Cambridge
1.23: Eric Keller, Sylvia T. Warner (2002) *Conversation Gambits* Cambridge
1.24: Michael J. Wallace. (2004) *Study Skills in English* Cambridge

Introductory comment

This is an introduction to the field of energy and introduces the idea that some different kinds of energy exist:
Energy.

Exercise 1

a) Read the notes below on the emerging use of biomass material.

1. Changing oil to biomass not easy – needs change in public attitude
2. Energy infrastructure centred on fossil fuel
3. Oil supply chains well established
4. Biomass use/supply chains not developed
5. Biomass problems: smoke/smell
6. Biomass difficult to use outside industry – specialist equipment needed
7. Biomass releases CO_2 into the atmosphere – effect carbon neutral – gas taken up earlier by plants
8. Burning organic material now more cost-effective – but downside
9. Wood pellets for heating now cheaper than heating oil or liquefied petroleum gases in the UK
10. Ethanol now cheaper than petrol
11. Burning biomass reduces greenhouse gas emissions by more than 90%
12. Biomass – various forms
13. Farming crops for fuel – next big change in agriculture
14. Hydrogen fuel cell buses piloted in London
15. Power stations experimenting with biomass plus fossil fuels
16. Ethanol easy biomass to use – added to petrol and used in cars
17. Ethanol fermented from plants high in sugar
18. Other forms of biomass: cow-dung, chicken litter and bedding, olive oil cake, methane from agricultural waste

b) Read the draft below explaining the emerging market in burning organic material, biomass, to produce energy, and set out some of the advantages and disadvantages.

c) Match the notes with the text. Underline the relevant text and write the corresponding number.

Some people say that the need for alternative sources of energy will change agriculture in the United Kingdom like coal did during the industrial revolution. Farmers are turning production away from food to growing crops that can produce biomass energy. Biomass has a variety of forms, and the two important ones are woody material like willow and miscanthus, which grow fast and can be easily burnt, and oil like sunflower oil, soy and palm oil, which has a high calorific value when burnt. An instance is ethanol, which can easily be fermented from grain or sugar and can be mixed with petrol in the ratio of one part ethanol and nine parts petrol. Also, ethanol doesn't need the vehicle to be changed when it is used in cars. Other forms of biomass are cow-dung, chicken litter and bedding, olive oil cake and methane from agricultural waste like manure, used cooking oil wood and pellets, which are now proving cheaper energy alternatives.

Although using biomass has many benefits, there are several major arguments against using fuel produced from biomass. The main one is that both the transport system and the whole energy infrastructure are organized around the use of fossil fuel. And, biomass oils like palm oil and wood from biomass materials can cause unpleasant smells and smoke. Bio-fuels can be difficult to use outside industry, as the supply of biomass and development of the necessary specialist equipment are in their infancy. And a shift in people's perception is required if using biomass is to take off.

However, the pressure from fuel shortages and cost can only exercise the minds of companies and encourage them to look for alternative energy sources. This is already happening as car companies increase the production of hybrid cars which run on a combination of oil and ethanol, fuel cell buses for urban transport and power stations mixing biomass like wood pellets with fossil fuels to produce energy. Some companies

Key:

Exercise 1

All of the points are mentioned except: 3, 4, 7, 8, 9, 10, 11. Part of 3 and 4 are used.

Exercise 2

Look at the paragraph below. You can see that parts of the text are crossed out. Which other parts of the text can you remove to create a brief summary of the paragraph? Compare your answer with the key.

~~It has been said that~~ the need for alternative ~~sources of~~ energy is ~~the driving force~~ behind a revolution, which is about to transform agriculture in the United Kingdom ~~in much the same way~~ as coal did during the industrial revolution. Farmers are turning ~~production away from food~~ to ~~growing~~ crops ~~that can be easily harvested~~ to provide biomass energy. Biomass has a variety of forms, of which the two main sources are; woody material like willow and miscanthus, which grow fast and can be easily burnt, and oil like sunflower oil, soy and palm oil, which has a high calorific value when burnt. Another good example is ethanol, which can easily be fermented from grain or sugar and can be mixed with petrol in the ratio of one part ethanol and nine parts petrol. Further, ethanol has the distinct of advantage of not requiring vehicle modification when it is used in cars. Other forms of biomass are cow-dung, chicken litter and bedding, olive oil cake and methane from agricultural waste like manure, used cooking oil wood pellets, all of which are now proving cheaper energy alternatives.

Key Exercise 2

~~It has been said that~~ the need for alternative ~~sources of~~ energy is ~~the driving force~~ behind a revolution, which is about to transform agriculture in the United Kingdom ~~in much the same way~~ as coal did during the industrial revolution. Farmers are turning ~~production away from food~~ to ~~growing~~ crops ~~that can be easily harvested~~ to provide biomass energy. Biomass has a variety of forms, ~~of which the two main sources are~~ woody material ~~like willow and miscanthus, which grow fast and can be easily burnt,~~ and oil ~~like sunflower oil, soy and palm oil,~~ which has a high calorific value ~~when burnt~~. ~~Another good example is~~ ethanol, ~~which~~ can easily be fermented from grain or sugar and can be mixed with petrol ~~in the ratio of one part ethanol and nine parts petrol~~. ~~Further,~~ ethanol has the ~~distinct~~ of advantage of not requiring vehicle modification ~~when it is used in cars~~. Other forms of biomass are cow-dung, chicken litter and bedding, ~~olive oil cake and methane from agricultural waste like manure, used cooking oil, wood pellets, all of which are now proving cheaper energy alternatives.~~

Exercise 3

a) Re-draft the text in bold below in your own words.
b) Re-draft the text using the items in the list below.

¹ **Some people say that** the need for alternative sources of energy ² **will change** agriculture in the United Kingdom ³ **like coal did** during the industrial revolution. Farmers are turning production away from food to growing crops ⁴ **that can produce** biomass energy. Biomass has a variety of forms, ⁵ **and the two important ones** are woody material like willow and miscanthus, which grow fast and can be easily burnt, and oil like sunflower oil, soy and palm oil, which has a high calorific value when burnt. ⁶ **An instance** is ethanol, which can easily be fermented from grain or sugar and can be mixed with petrol in the ratio of one part ethanol and nine parts petrol. ⁷ **Also**, ethanol ⁸ **doesn't need the vehicle to be changed** when it is used in cars. Other forms of biomass are cow-dung, chicken litter and bedding, olive oil cake and methane from agricultural waste like manure, used cooking oil wood pellets, ⁹ **which** are now proving cheaper energy alternatives.

¹⁰ **Although using biomass has many benefits**, there are several major arguments against using fuel produced from biomass. ¹¹ **The main one is that** both the transport system and the whole energy infrastructure are organized around the use of fossil fuel. ¹² **And**, biomass oils like palm oil and wood from biomass materials can cause unpleasant smells and smoke. Bio-fuels can be difficult to use outside industry, as the supply of biomass and development of the necessary specialist equipment are in their infancy. ¹³ **And** a shift in people's perception is required if using biomass is to take off.

However, the pressure from fuel shortages and cost can only exercise the minds of companies and encourage them to look for alternative energy sources. ¹⁴ **This** is already happening ¹⁵ **as car companies increase the production** of hybrid cars which run on a combination of oil and ethanol, fuel cell buses for urban transport and power stations mixing biomass like wood pellets with fossil fuels to produce energy. Some companies are already burning rubbish to produce energy and using methane, or so called landfill gas, from rubbish sites. So, the revolution has already commenced.

Redrafting items

a. foremost among these is the fact that
b. In spite of the obvious advantages to the environment of burning organic material to produce energy,
c. moreover
d. with car manufacturers now increasing the production of or introducing
e. an added problem is that
f. all of which
g. has the distinct of advantage of not requiring vehicle modification
h. that can be easily harvested to provide
i. is the driving force behind a revolution, which is about to transform
k. further
l. It has been said that
m. there are signs that this
n. another good example is
o. in much the same way as coal did
p. of which the two main sources

KEY for Exercise 3.

It has been said that the need for alternative sources of energy **is the driving force behind a revolution, which is about to transform** agriculture in the United Kingdom **in much the same way as coal** did during the industrial revolution. Farmers are turning production away from food to growing crops **that can be easily harvested to provide** biomass energy. Biomass has a variety of forms, **of which the two main sources** are woody material like willow and miscanthus, which grow fast and can be easily burnt, and oil like sunflower oil, soy and palm oil, which has a high calorific value when burnt. **Another good example is** ethanol, which can easily be fermented from grain or sugar and can be mixed with petrol in the ratio of one part ethanol and nine parts petrol. **Further**, ethanol **has the distinct of advantage of not requiring vehicle modification** when it is used in cars. Other forms of biomass are cow-dung, chicken litter and bedding, olive oil cake and methane from agricultural waste like manure, used cooking oil wood pellets, **all of which** are now proving cheaper energy alternatives.

In spite of the obvious advantages to the environment of burning organic material to produce energy, there are several major arguments against using fuel produced from biomass. **Foremost among these is the fact that** both the transport system and the whole energy infrastructure are organised around the use of fossil fuel. **Moreover**, biomass oils like palm oil and wood from organic materials can cause unpleasant smells and smoke. Bio-fuels can also be difficult to use outside industry, as the supply of biomass and development of the necessary specialist equipment are in their infancy. **An added problem is that** a shift in people's perception is required if using biomass is to take off.

However, the pressure from fuel shortages and cost can only exercise the minds of companies and encourage them to look for alternative energy sources. **There are signs that this** is already happening **with car manufacturers now increasing the production of or introducing** hybrid cars which run on a combination of oil and ethanol, fuel cell buses for urban transport and power stations mixing biomass like wood pellets with fossil fuels to produce energy. Some companies are already burning rubbish to produce energy and using methane, or so called landfill gas, from rubbish sites. So, the revolution has already commenced.

Exercise 4.

In the text below some words and phrases have been covered. Reconstruct the text.

It has been said that the need for alternative sources of energy is the driving force behind a revolution, which is _____ put to transform agricu_____ _____ the United Kingdom in much t_____ way as coal d_____ _____ing the industr_____ _____ Farmers are turning prod_____ _____ from food t_____ _____ing crops _____ it can be _____ _____rvested to provide biomass _____ Biomass has a _____ riety of f_____, of which the _____ main s_____ ces are woody mate_____ _____ke willow and miscanth_____ _____ch grow fast and can _____ _____ily burnt, and oil like_____ _____ower oil, soy and pa_____ _____ has a high ca_____ _____alue when burnt. Another good example is ethanol_____ _____ _____ily be ferme_____ _____ in or sugar and can be mixed with petrol i_____ _____e ratio of one part ethan_____ _____ parts petrol. Further, ethanol ha_____ the distinct advantage of not re_____ _____g _____ehicle modificati_____ _____t is use_____ in _____ars. Other forms of biomass are cow-dung, ch_____cken litter and b_____ _____ olive oil _____ methane from agricultural waste like manure, used coo_____ _____ wood pe_____ _____ of which are now proving cheaper energy alternatives.

In spite _____ the obvious _____ _____ the environment of burning organic material to produce _____rgy, there _____ _____ajor arguments against us_____ _____ roduced from bio_____ _____oremost among _____ _____s the fact that both the transp_____ _____stem and the whole_____ _____y infrastructu_____ _____ ed around the use _____ _____reover, bio_____ _____e palm oi_____ _____om organi_____ _____aterials can cau_____ _____easant sm_____ _____. Bio-fue_____ _____ _____ be di_____ _____ use outside ind_____ _____s the su_____ of biomass and dev_____ _____ent _____f the n_____ _____ary specialist equipment are in th_____ _____fancy. An add_____ _____ is that a shi_____ in _____ple's perception is required if using biomass is to take off.

However, the pr_____ _____ure from fuel shortages and cost can only exerc_____ _____inds of companies an_____ _____ncourage them to look for _____ _____e energy sour_____ _____here are signs tha_____ _____is already happening _____ _____ufacturers no_____ _____ing the product_____ _____ _____ducing hybrid cars _____ _____ a combination_____ oil and ethanol _____ _____es for urban transp_____ _____ _____tations mixing biomass like wood pe_____ _____ fossil fuels to produce e_____ _____. _____ ne companies are already burning ru_____ _____ to _____roduce energy _____ _____, or so called landfill gas, from rubbi_____ _____ _____olution has already commenced.

Key: Exercise 4

See the text in Exercise 2.

Exercise 5

Put the jumbled texts 1–11 into the correct order.

1. sources of energy is the driving force behind a revolution, which

2. mixed with petrol in the ratio of one part ethanol and nine parts petrol. Further, ethanol has the distinct of advantage of not requiring

3. vehicle modification when it is used in cars. Other forms of biomass are cow-dung, chicken litter and bedding, olive oil cake and methane from

4. is about to transform agriculture in the United Kingdom in much the same

5. willow and miscanthus, which grow fast and can be easily burnt, and oil like sunflower oil, soy and palm oil, which

6. harvested to provide biomass energy. Biomass has a variety of forms, of which the two main sources are woody material like

7. way as coal did during the industrial revolution. Farmers are

8. agricultural waste like manure, used cooking oil wood pellets, all of which are now proving cheaper energy alternatives.

9. turning production away from food to growing crops that can be easily

10. has a high calorific value when burnt. Another good example is ethanol, which can easily be fermented from grain or sugar and can be

11. It has been said that the need for alternative

Exercise 9
Correct order: 11, 1, 4, 7, 9, 6, 5, 10, 2, 3, 8

SKILLS	OBJECTIVES
Integrated Skills	To discuss points for and against an issue To understand definitions in context To locate topic sentences and points in an argument To use staging in a written argument To listen for meaning and content
Writing	To practise writing extended argumentative texts To practise making generalisations To practise writing definitions, giving examples and classifying information
Reading	To read and analyse the features of comparative/contrastive texts To practise reading and describing graphs
Listening	To practise listening for and recording numbers in texts To practise listening for connectives and sequence markers to assist comprehension To practise listening and note taking in preparation for discussion
Speaking	To listen to and practise small group discussion skills
Study Skills	To practise using dictionary for pronunciation and vocab extension
Assessment	Report – First draft due

Key references for further study

Reading activity

Selected reading

Unit 4. EAP Now! Preliminary. Kathy Cox & David Hill. 2007.

Reading 1. HHO gas, also known as oxyhydrogen can greatly increase the fuel efficiency of cars in which it is used. HHO gas is created through a simple process of electrolysis - the car does not run just on HHO but rather a hybrid of gasoline and HHO which powers the car. HHO has been shown to increase fuel efficiency by as much as 60% in some cases.

HHO is a hydrogen/oxygen compound, in a two to one ratio. This is of course the same proportion as found in water. Combustion is a process in which something is burned in order to release heat energy and begins when a substance is heated to its autoignition threshold. This is the temperature at which a given substance will spontaneously ignite with no external source of flame needed. The autoignition temperature of HHO is 1065 degrees Fahrenheit and the amount of energy which would be required for this to happen is 20 microjoules. After being ingnited, HHO is converted to water vapor and also releases energy, which sustains this reaction.

One common usage of HHO is in torches which are used ion the manufacturing processes of refractory material. Limelights are another application of HHO (which is sometimes used in lamps), where light is produced by heating lime. HHO can be explosive and for this reason, limelights have for the most part been phased out in favor of electric lighting. More recently, HHO has been pressed into service helping cars to run on water. There are many manuals on doing this conversion available online which can give you step by step instructions in making your own HHO kits and installing them in your vehicle. When talking about the automotive applications of HHO it is often called Brown gas.

Water will be stored under the hood of the vehicle and ignited by a spark form the car battery. The electrolysis of the water stored in the car will then begin and HHO or Brown gas will be produced as a result. The air intake valve of the car's engine will pull this gas into the combustion chamber. When mixed with gasoline, this Brown gas gives vehicles dramatically better gas mileage.

It is a simple matter to make and install your own HHO kit for your vehicle - this does not require any specialized knowledge; you don't need to know the first thing about cars to be successful in installing a HHO kit!

Ryan Edward and his team have reviewed all of the so-called best of the best, HHO Gas Generator Guides on the market. He shares their findings and shows you the results from their extensive HHO Gas Generator Guides Reviews at his website. To visit Ryan's website now please click on the following link...

Go To: http://www.RyseReviews.com/HHO/

Article Source: http://EzineArticles.com/?expert=Ryan_Edward

References

Module 5 Communication

Module Overview

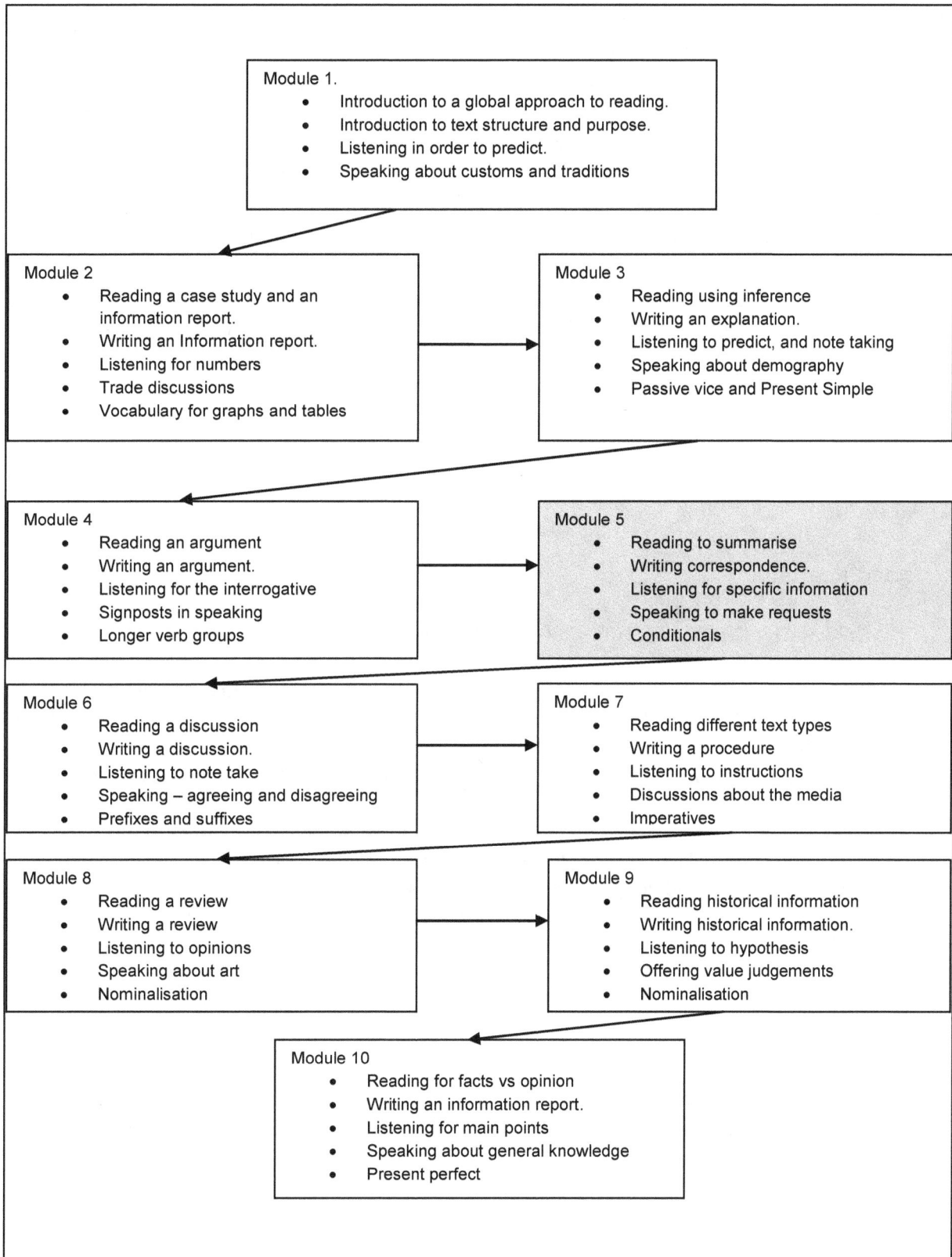

Module 1.
- Introduction to a global approach to reading.
- Introduction to text structure and purpose.
- Listening in order to predict.
- Speaking about customs and traditions

Module 2
- Reading a case study and an information report.
- Writing an Information report.
- Listening for numbers
- Trade discussions
- Vocabulary for graphs and tables

Module 3
- Reading using inference
- Writing an explanation.
- Listening to predict, and note taking
- Speaking about demography
- Passive vice and Present Simple

Module 4
- Reading an argument
- Writing an argument.
- Listening for the interrogative
- Signposts in speaking
- Longer verb groups

Module 5
- Reading to summarise
- Writing correspondence.
- Listening for specific information
- Speaking to make requests
- Conditionals

Module 6
- Reading a discussion
- Writing a discussion.
- Listening to note take
- Speaking – agreeing and disagreeing
- Prefixes and suffixes

Module 7
- Reading different text types
- Writing a procedure
- Listening to instructions
- Discussions about the media
- Imperatives

Module 8
- Reading a review
- Writing a review
- Listening to opinions
- Speaking about art
- Nominalisation

Module 9
- Reading historical information
- Writing historical information.
- Listening to hypothesis
- Offering value judgements
- Nominalisation

Module 10
- Reading for facts vs opinion
- Writing an information report.
- Listening for main points
- Speaking about general knowledge
- Present perfect

Module Objectives

Following completion of this module, you should be able to:

- Know more vocabulary for talking about communication
- Be more fluent in talking about communication
- Have further practised reading for main ideas and reading for detail
- Be aware of the differences in formatting and language between informal emails, formal emails and formal letters
- Have further practised listening for specific information
- Know more vocabulary on the topic of telephoning
- Have improved accuracy in using conditional expressions for real possibilities
- Have practised making telephone enquiries
- Have improved accuracy, skill and ability to adjust the level of politeness in making requests

Learning resources

Selected Readings:

1.25: Kathy Cox. David Hill. (2004) *EAP Now! Preliminary*. Pearson Education Australia
1.26: R.R.Jordan. (2007) *New Edition Academic Writing Course*. Longman
1.27: Karen Blanchard. Christine Root. *Ready to Write More: From Paragraph to Essay*. Longman
1.28: Jack C. Richards, Samuela Eckstut-Didier. (2009) *Strategic Reading 2* Cambridge.
1.29: Helen Solorzano, Laurie Frazier. (2009) *Contemporary Topics 1-2*. Longman
1.30: Steven Gershon (2008*) Present Yourself 2: Viewpoints* Cambridge
1.31: Eric Keller, Sylvia T. Warner (2002) *Conversation Gambits* Cambridge
1.32: Michael J. Wallace. (2004) *Study Skills in English* Cambridge

Introductory comment

Many people think that communicating is nothing more that talking a lot and speaking clearly. However, in reality, good communication is far more complicated than that.
Communication.

Module 5

SKILLS	OBJECTIVES
Integrated Skills	To discuss main ideas and specific information To write formal and informal e-mails To listen for specific information in telephone conversations
Writing	To practise planning and writing texts that describe causes and effects To practise presenting quantitative and symbolic information in assignments e.g. tables, graphs and graphics
Reading	To read and analyse the features of comparative/contrastive texts To practise reading and describing graphs
Listening	To practise listening for and recording numbers in texts To practise listening for connectives and sequence markers to assist comprehension To practise listening and note taking in preparation for discussion
Speaking	To listen to and practise small group discussion skills
Study Skills	Essay Presentation To practise acknowledging sources of information in assignments
Assessment	Report – Submit Final draft
Tests	Listening, Reading and Writing tests

Exercises

Your beliefs about communication

How can you learn to become a better communicator?

Do you think the following statements are true or false?

• Good communicators in their own language are usually good communicators in other languages too

• Body language, gestures and facial expressions are more important than the words you use

• Most gestures are the same in every country

• It's always important to keep eye contact while

• Using too many gestures to communicate in another language makes communicating too easy and so stops your speech developing

• Good communication cannot be taught

• You can learn to interpret people's body language

• I would notice if someone was mirroring (copying people's body language to make them feel sympathetic to you) and feel uncomfortable

• Being a good listener is more important than being a fluent speaker

• You can learn to be a good listener

Compare answers with your partner, and say why you have that opinion

Are there any points you would like to discuss as a class, for example ones you still aren't sure about?

What are the most important things about being a good communicator?

Telephoning match the conversations pairwork

Worksheet 1- Match the dialogues

Student A

Without showing your worksheet to your partner, match your 4 half dialogues to your partner's (which are in a different order)
Conversation 1

A: Hello, Plus One News. How can I help you?

B: _____

A: Ah, hello Mr Smith. Mr Johnson is waiting for your call. I'll just check if he's available. Please hold the line.

B: _____

A: Mr Johnson?

B: _____

A: I'm afraid Mr Johnson is on another line. Shall I put you through to his secretary?

B: _____

Conversation 2

A: Hello. Plus One News. Jane speaking.

B: _____

A: Can I ask what it is concerning?

B: _____

A: You need to speak to our Mediterranean correspondent, Mr Johnson. Shall I put you through to him now?

B: _____

A: Okay. Please hold the line.

B: _____

Conversation 3

A: Hello.

B: _____

A: No, I'm sorry. This is Mama Mia Pizza Delivery. You must have dialed the wrong number.

B: _____

A: Of course. Go ahead.

B: _____

A: No, this is seven three double oh four two four.

B: _____

Conversation 4

A: Plus One News Limited. Jane Smithers speaking. How can I help you?

B: _____

A: Oh, hi John. How are you?

B: _____

A: Not bad. Mr Johnson always keeps me busy too.

B: _____

A: I think so. Just hold the line for a second and I'll check.

B: _____

(Optional) Fill in the gaps with your partner's half of each dialogue.
Telephoning match the conversations pairwork

Worksheet 1- Match the dialogues

Student B

Without showing your worksheet to your partner, match your 4 half dialogues to your partner's (which are in a different order)
Conversation A

A:
_____

B: Hello. Is that Plus One News?

A: _____

B: Oh, I'm terribly sorry. Can I just check if I have the right number?

A: _____

B: Is that seven double three oh four two four?

A: _____

B: Oh, I do apologize. I'll try and dial the number again.

Conversation B

A:
_____

B: Hello, this is John Smith calling from the Big Ben News Agency.

A: _____

B: Okay. Thank you.

A: _____

B: Yes.

A: _____

B: Yes please.

Conversation C

A:
_____

B: Hi Jane, it's John.

A: _____

B: Very well, but a bit busy since I was transferred to the Middle East. How's everything with you?

A: _____

B: Is he available at the moment, do you know?

A: _____

B: Cheers.

Conversation D

A:

_____

B: Hello. Can I speak to someone on your foreign affairs desk please?

A: _____

B: I have some information about the situation in the Straits of Gibraltar.

A: _____

B: Yes please.

A: _____

B: Okay, thank you.

(Optional) Fill in the gaps with your partner's half of each dialogue.
Worksheet 2- Partial Answers and Can/ Will/ Shall Exercises
Check your answers from Worksheet 1 below (don't worry about the gaps for now)

A: Hello, Plus One News. How _____ I help you?

B: Hello, this is John Smith calling from the Big Ben News Agency.

A: Ah, hello Mr Smith. Mr Johnson is waiting for your call. I _____ just check if he's available. Please hold the line.

B: Okay. Thank you.

A: Mr Johnson?

B: Yes.

A: I'm afraid Mr Johnson is on another line. _____ I put you through to his secretary?

B: Yes please.

A: Hello. Plus One News. Jane speaking.

B: Hello. _____ I speak to someone on your foreign affairs desk please?

A: _____ I ask what it is concerning?

B: I have some information about the situation in the Straits of Gibraltar.

A: You need to speak to our Mediterranean correspondent, Mr Johnson. _____ I put you through to him now?

B: Yes please.

A: Okay. Please hold the line.

B: Okay, thank you.

A: Hello.

B: Hello. Is that Plus One News?

A: No, I'm sorry. This is Mama Mia Pizza Delivery. You must have dialed the wrong number.

B: Oh, I'm terribly sorry. _____ I just check if I have the right number?

A: Of course. Go ahead.

B: Is that seven double three oh four two four?

A: No, this is seven three double oh four two four.

B: Oh, I do apologize. I _____ try and dial the number again.

A: Plus One News Limited. Jane Smithers speaking. How _____ I help you?

B: Hi Jane, it's John.

A: Oh, hi John. How are you?

B: Very well, but a bit busy since I was transferred to the Middle East. How's everything with you?

A: Not bad. Mr Johnson always keeps me busy too.

B: Is he available at the moment, do you know?

A: I think so. Just hold the line for a second and I_____ check.

B: Cheers.

Without looking back at Worksheet 1, try to fill the following gaps with the correct form with "can", "will" or "shall".

Worksheet 3 – Full answer key

Check your answers from Worksheet 2 below

A: Hello, Plus One News. How can I help you?

B: Hello, this is John Smith calling from the Big Ben News Agency.

A: Ah, hello Mr Smith. Mr Johnson is waiting for your call. I'll just check if he's available. Please hold the line.

B: Okay. Thank you.

A: Mr Johnson?

B: Yes.

A: I'm afraid Mr Johnson is on another line. Shall I put you through to his secretary?

B: Yes please.

A: Hello. Plus One News. Jane speaking.

B: Hello. Can I speak to someone on your foreign affairs desk please?

A: Can I ask what it is concerning?

B: I have some information about the situation in the Straits of Gibraltar.

A: You need to speak to our Mediterranean correspondent, Mr Johnson. Shall I put you through to him now?

B: Yes please.

A: Okay. Please hold the line.

B: Okay, thank you.

A: Hello.

B: Hello. Is that Plus One News?

A: No, I'm sorry. This is Mama Mia Pizza Delivery. You must have dialed the wrong number.

B: Oh, I'm terribly sorry. Can I just check if I have the right number?

A: Of course. Go ahead.

B: Is that seven double three oh four two four?

A: No, this is seven three double oh four two four.

B: Oh, I do apologize. I'll try and dial the number again.

A: Plus One News Limited. Jane Smithers speaking. How can I help you?

B: Hi Jane, it's John.

A: Oh, hi John. How are you?

B: Very well, but a bit busy since I was transferred to the Middle East. How's everything with you?

A: Not bad. Mr Johnson always keeps me busy too.

B: Is he available at the moment, do you know?

A: I think so. Just hold the line for a second and I'll check.

B: Cheers.

Practice the dialogues in pairs.

Practice more times, covering more and more of the bottom of the conversation each time. You don't have to use exactly the same words as is there, but you do have to successfully finish the conversation each time.

List of phrasal verbs used for telephoning

Hold on = hang on
Go on = go ahead
Put you through (= connect you)
Look it up
Look for
Get through
Hang up
Get back to me/ someone
Tied up (= busy)
Off the hook
Cut off
Call/ phone someone back
Read something back
Check something back
Speak up
Pick up

Key references for further study

Reading activity

Selected reading

Unit 5. EAP Now! Preliminary. Kathy Cox & David Hill. 2007.

References

Module 6 Politics

Module Overview

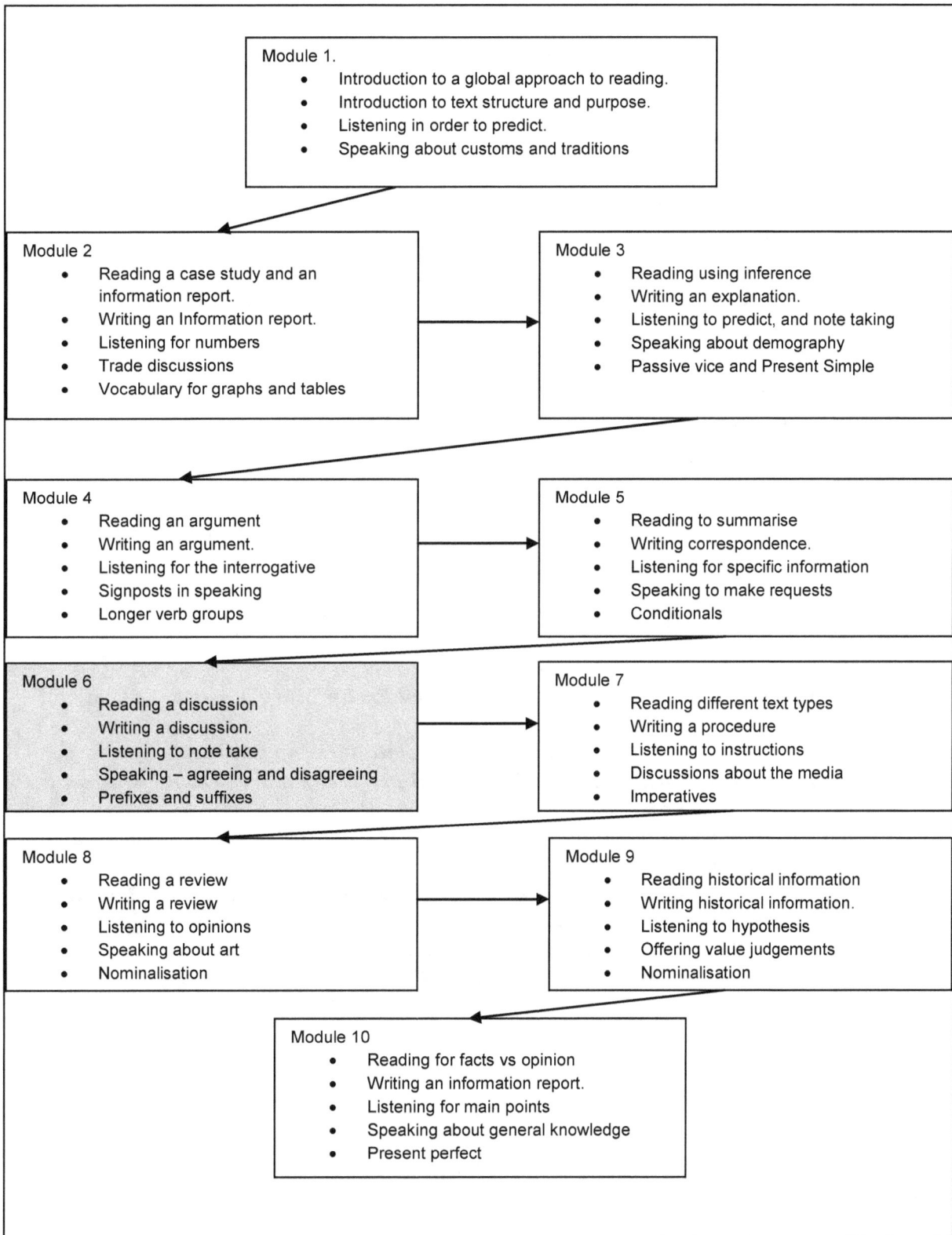

Module 1.
- Introduction to a global approach to reading.
- Introduction to text structure and purpose.
- Listening in order to predict.
- Speaking about customs and traditions

Module 2
- Reading a case study and an information report.
- Writing an Information report.
- Listening for numbers
- Trade discussions
- Vocabulary for graphs and tables

Module 3
- Reading using inference
- Writing an explanation.
- Listening to predict, and note taking
- Speaking about demography
- Passive vice and Present Simple

Module 4
- Reading an argument
- Writing an argument.
- Listening for the interrogative
- Signposts in speaking
- Longer verb groups

Module 5
- Reading to summarise
- Writing correspondence.
- Listening for specific information
- Speaking to make requests
- Conditionals

Module 6
- Reading a discussion
- Writing a discussion.
- Listening to note take
- Speaking – agreeing and disagreeing
- Prefixes and suffixes

Module 7
- Reading different text types
- Writing a procedure
- Listening to instructions
- Discussions about the media
- Imperatives

Module 8
- Reading a review
- Writing a review
- Listening to opinions
- Speaking about art
- Nominalisation

Module 9
- Reading historical information
- Writing historical information.
- Listening to hypothesis
- Offering value judgements
- Nominalisation

Module 10
- Reading for facts vs opinion
- Writing an information report.
- Listening for main points
- Speaking about general knowledge
- Present perfect

Module Objectives

Following completion of this module, you should be able to:

> Recognise a prefix and a suffix
> Know how to critically examine an issue like war and be able to express an opinion
> Be able to recognise features of individual paragraphs within a longer text
> Understand some of the features of a discussion essay
> Be able to map an essay
> Be able to use modality and present simple tense when talking about future predictions
> Understand probability; possibility; certainty and the language that they signal
> Have practised agreeing and disagreeing
> Have listened for and recognised some importance markers based on intonation, stress and emphasis of the speaker

Learning resources

Selected Readings:

1.33: Kathy Cox. David Hill. (2004) *EAP Now! Preliminary*. Pearson Education Australia
1.34: R.R.Jordan. (2007) *New Edition Academic Writing Course*. Longman
1.35: Karen Blanchard. Christine Root. *Ready to Write More: From Paragraph to Essay*. Longman
1.36: Jack C. Richards, Samuela Eckstut-Didier. (2009) *Strategic Reading 2* Cambridge.
1.37: Helen Solorzano, Laurie Frazier. (2009) *Contemporary Topics 1-2*. Longman
1.38: Steven Gershon (2008*) Present Yourself 2: Viewpoints* Cambridge
1.39: Eric Keller, Sylvia T. Warner (2002) *Conversation Gambits* Cambridge
1.40: Michael J. Wallace. (2004) *Study Skills in English* Cambridge

Introductory comment

It is often said that people should never discuss politics or religion. It may be because discussions of this nature might begin as pleasant conversations but then become heated arguments:
Politics.

Politics: Political Systems Text maze

Read the paragraph below and find the text in the maze.

P	o	l	i	t	o	m	m	u	n	i	s	m	f	o	t	r	o	l	l
c	o	a	r	i	C	t	h	g	i	e	h	t	m	r	n	a	F	d	e
e	n	n	c	c	a	l	s	y	r	f	f	t	o	e	o	s	c	i	s
e	o	o	h	l	i	t	i	s	r	a	e	t	r	x	c	e	e	s	m
h	m	m	y	o	h	t	c	t	a	r	l	o	f	a	y	k	s	t	o
t	y	A	i	p	a	i	a	e	f	e	h	t	e	m	l	r	i	c	o
d	h	w	s	l	n	w	l	m	s	r	a	n	g	p	n	e		h	r
n	e	n	a	l	i	d	p	o	w	e	r	i	s	l	o	h			g
a	i	v	i	d	n	e	g	d	n	i	l	e	a	e	m	t			a
m	d	u	a	l	C	a	p	o	a	m	y	t	b	i	m	y	z	i	n
e	t	s	e	m	e	h	i	l	l	o	o	u	s	s	o	b	e	a	n
h	a	y	a	e	r	t	t	y	l	n	r	l	o	a	c	d	e	n	a
c	s	s	n	v	i	n	a	s	l	a	i	c	o	s	s	i	y	w	t
u	t	l	s	e	s	e	l	t	a	s	s	e	s	a	r	e	t	o	i
s	h	a	o	w	w	h	i	r	l	c	h	c	i	h	w	a	r	y	o
s	e	c	f	o	h	m	s	u	c	t	u	r	e	i	n	b	e	l	n
m	p	i	p	r	o	d	u	c	t	i	e	h	s	i	l	o	p	e	o
e	o	t	i	c	e	p	s	r	o	d	a	n	d	p	r	o	t	n
t	l	i	v	e	s	v	a	l	e	n	a	r	e	p	r	i	v	a	c
s	y	s	d	n	a	s	e	u	p	t	s	i	t	a	r	o	p	r	o

Find the text in the maze!

Political systems range from the far left to the far right. Communism for example is a social structure in which classes are abolished and property is commonly controlled. Fascism seeks to organize a nation on corporatist perspectives, values, and systems such as the political system and the economy. A monarchy is when all political power is absolutely or nominally lodged with an individual. Capitalism however is when the means of production are privately owned by the rich.

1. What is a monarchy? _____
2. What is communism? _____
3. What political system is used in your country? _____
4. What are the differences between facism and capitalism? _____
_____

Political Vocabulary Puzzle

Read the clues and then complete the puzzle.

He is _____

He is a _____

Across: →

1. A system of government marked by centralization of authority under a dictator. _____

4. One who is actively involved in politics, especially party politics. _____

9. The act of constituting or state of being constituted. _____

10. A public vote on an official proposition. _____

Down: ↓

2. A state ruled or headed by a monarch. _____

3. A system of government in which the state plans and controls the economy. _____

5. An economic system in which the means of production are privately owned. _____

6. A system of government where political sovereignty is retained by the people. _____

7. A political organization. _____

8. A preference, such as a raised hand or a marked ballot. _____

Teacher's answers

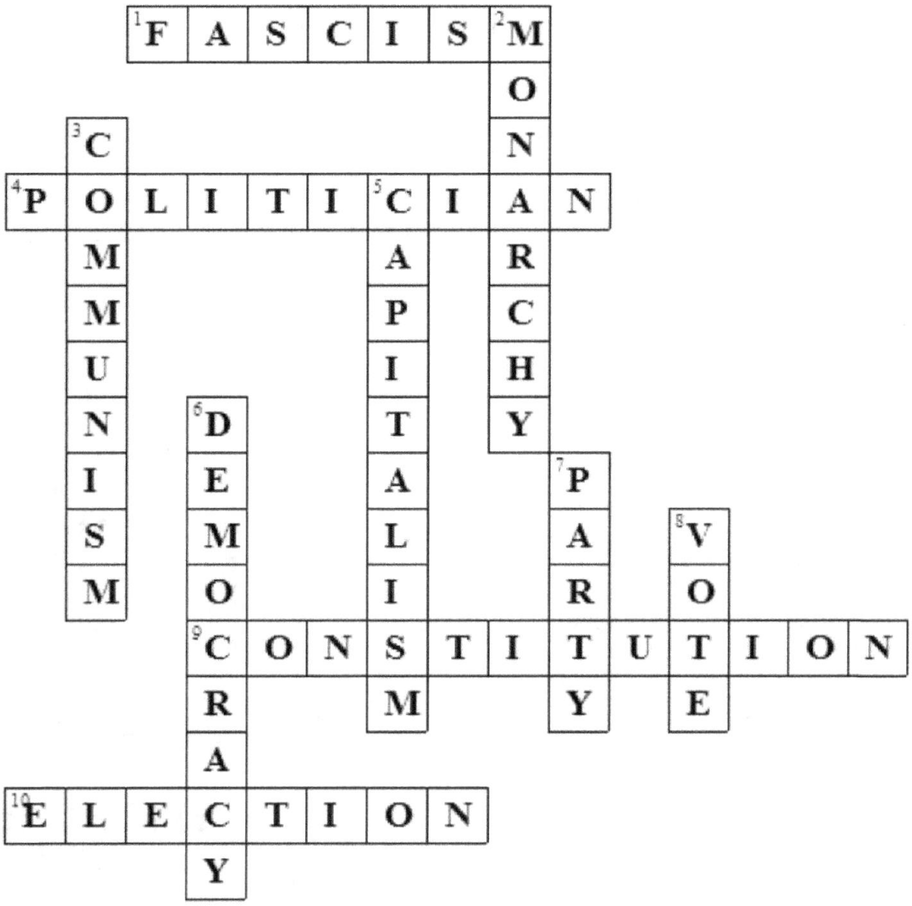
1 FASCISM
2 MONARCHY
3 COMMUNISM
4 POLITICIAN
5 CAPITALISM
6 DEMOCRACY
7 PARTY
8 VOTE
9 CONSTITUTION
10 ELECTION

Modal Verbs - Using Must + More or less

Name: _____   Date: _____

Complete the worksheet using the correct modal verb and adjective.

1) My teeth are bad. You _____ brush your teeth _____.

a) must   b) mustn't   c) more   d) less

2) I'm always in trouble at school. You _____ play _____ in class.

a) must   b) mustn't   c) more   d) less

3) He's always tired. He must get _____ sleep.

a) must   b) mustn't   c) more   d) less

4) She drinks too much coffee. She _____ drink _____ water.

a) must   b) mustn't   c) more   d) less

5) They're too fat. They must eat _____ sugar.

a) must   b) mustn't   c) more   d) less

6) We _____ forget to do homework, if we want _____ gold stars.

a) must   b) mustn't   c) more   d) less

7) They _____ spend all their money, if they want to buy _____ presents.

a) must   b) mustn't   c) more   d) less

Modal Verbs: What should and shouldn't you do?

Complete the worksheet by explaining what you did in the past.

What should you drink? ⟶ Tom said you should drink water because it's healthy.
What shouldn't you drink? ⟶ Tom said you shouldn't drink soda because it's unhealthy.

Questions	Classmates
What should you eat?	
What shouldn't you eat?	
What should you do at school?	
What shouldn't you do at school?	
What should you wear in the winter?	
What shouldn't you wear in the winter?	
What should you do at home?	
What shouldn't you do at home?	

Module 6

SKILLS	OBJECTIVES
Integrated Skills	To understand use of prefixes and suffixes To understand features of paragraphs To map out a discussion essay To listen and take notes
Writing	To obtain information through surveys and questionnaires To practise drawing conclusions including how to use information obtained in a questionnaire or survey
Reading	To practise scanning To practise reading for specific information To practise timed reading To consolidate work Weeks 1-5
Listening	To practise listening for and responding to directions and instructions To practise listening and note taking
Speaking	Oral presentation techniques
Study Skills	Essay presentation including formatting and title pages

Key references for further study

Reading activity

Selected reading

Unit 6. EAP Now! Preliminary. Kathy Cox & David Hill. 2007.

References

Module 7 Media

Module Overview

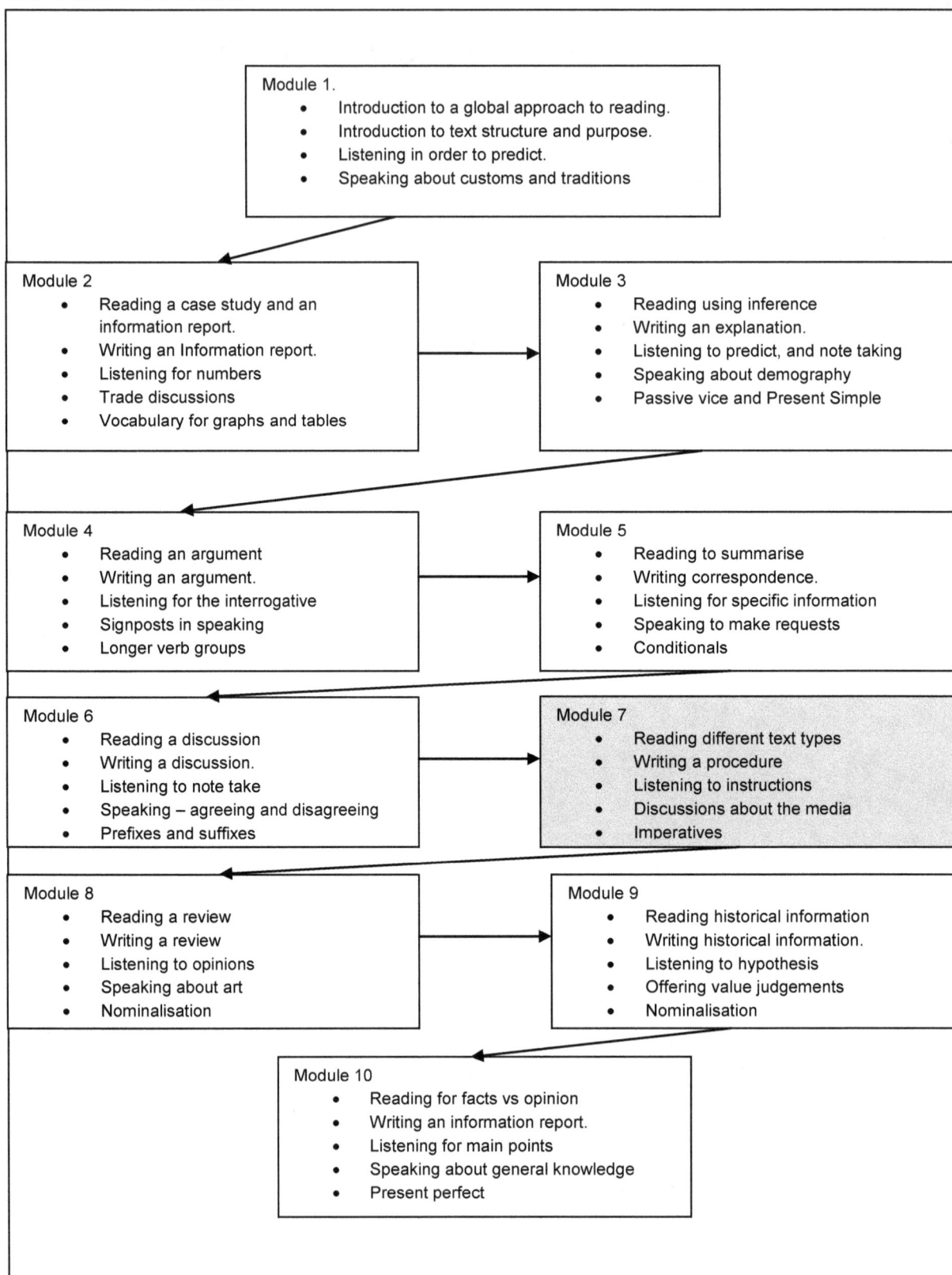

Module 1.
- Introduction to a global approach to reading.
- Introduction to text structure and purpose.
- Listening in order to predict.
- Speaking about customs and traditions

Module 2
- Reading a case study and an information report.
- Writing an Information report.
- Listening for numbers
- Trade discussions
- Vocabulary for graphs and tables

Module 3
- Reading using inference
- Writing an explanation.
- Listening to predict, and note taking
- Speaking about demography
- Passive vice and Present Simple

Module 4
- Reading an argument
- Writing an argument.
- Listening for the interrogative
- Signposts in speaking
- Longer verb groups

Module 5
- Reading to summarise
- Writing correspondence.
- Listening for specific information
- Speaking to make requests
- Conditionals

Module 6
- Reading a discussion
- Writing a discussion.
- Listening to note take
- Speaking – agreeing and disagreeing
- Prefixes and suffixes

Module 7
- Reading different text types
- Writing a procedure
- Listening to instructions
- Discussions about the media
- Imperatives

Module 8
- Reading a review
- Writing a review
- Listening to opinions
- Speaking about art
- Nominalisation

Module 9
- Reading historical information
- Writing historical information.
- Listening to hypothesis
- Offering value judgements
- Nominalisation

Module 10
- Reading for facts vs opinion
- Writing an information report.
- Listening for main points
- Speaking about general knowledge
- Present perfect

Module Objectives

Following completion of this module, you should be able to:

- ➤ Know more vocabulary for talking about the media
- ➤ Have increased fluency in talking about the media
- ➤ Have improved their skill at identifying different kinds of procedural text
- ➤ Be more aware of some forms of cohesion in English
- ➤ Be able to interpret some nominalisations
- ➤ Be able to use imperatives and other structures for giving instructions and advice
- ➤ Be able to write one kind of procedural text
- ➤ Be aware of one style of note-taking
- ➤ Have practised following and taking notes from a lecture

Learning resources

Selected Readings:

1.41: Kathy Cox. David Hill. (2004) *EAP Now! Preliminary*. Pearson Education Australia
1.42: R.R.Jordan. (2007) *New Edition Academic Writing Course*. Longman
1.43: Karen Blanchard. Christine Root. *Ready to Write More: From Paragraph to Essay*. Longman
1.44: Jack C. Richards, Samuela Eckstut-Didier. (2009) *Strategic Reading 2* Cambridge.
1.45: Helen Solorzano, Laurie Frazier. (2009) *Contemporary Topics 1-2*. Longman
1.46: Steven Gershon (2008*) Present Yourself 2: Viewpoints* Cambridge
1.47: Eric Keller, Sylvia T. Warner (2002) *Conversation Gambits* Cambridge
1.48: Michael J. Wallace. (2004) *Study Skills in English* Cambridge

Introductory comment

Many people think that communicating is nothing more that talking a lot and speaking clearly. However, in reality, good communication is far more complicated than that.
Media.

BBC Blue Planet: Animals and their Environment

Watch BBC Blue Planet and answer the questions. Now, click on the link below to access the video.

http://v.youku.com/v_show/id_XMzQwNTYxOTY=.html

1. What is the first animal you see?
_____

2. How long is the blue whale?
_____

3. How much of the Earth's surface is covered by water?
_____

4. What animal swims onto shore and eats a seal?
_____

5. What fish do the dolphins eat?
_____

6. How many sharks are there?
_____

7. What is the name of the bird that dives into the water?
_____

8. How many albatross birds are there?
_____

9. Which country do the turtles visit to lay their eggs?
_____

10. What animals eat the herring eggs?
_____

11. Which animal is trying to kill the whale calf?
_____

12. What animal mates from the deep sea?
_____

12. Now, write about a sea animal you like. Write 30 words.

BBC Planet Earth: Animals and their Environment

Watch BBC Planet Earth and answer the questions. Now, click on the link below to access the video.

http://v.youku.com/v_show/id_XMTI0MzAxMjYw.html

1. What part of the world do emperor penguins live in?

2. Describe the weather. Use five adjectives.

3. When will the emperor penguins see the sun again?

4. What animals are in the film? Name five.

5. What animal is in its den?

6. What is a young polar bear called?

7. What do polar bears like to eat?

8. What do you call it when animals move from one place to another each year?

9. What animal species is hunting the caribou?

10. How many Amur leopards are there left in their natural habitat?

11. What's the term we use to describe a species that has completely died?

12. What mammal is swimming off the coast of South Africa?

13. Which fish swims off the coast of South Africa?

14. How much of the world is covered by desert?

12. Now, write about an animal you like. Write 30 words.

Politics and Youth

Worksheet A – Political people and places.

1) This person is the head of the government.
2) This person is the head of state.
3) These people are elected to represent their areas (known as constituencies). They are also known as MPs.
4) This place is where the Parliament meets.
5) This is the name of the main right-wing party.
6) This is the name of the main left-wing party.

The Queen / The Conservative Party / The Prime Minister / Members of Parliament / The Houses of Parliament / The Labour Party

---

Worksheet B – Find Somebody Who...

Find somebody who...	Name	Extra information
... knows the name of the British Prime Minister.		
... would like to be a politician.		
... thinks that voting in elections is very important.		
... thinks there should be more women politicians in their country.		
... believes that most politicians are too old!		
... can name five politicians from their own country.		

Worksheet C – sentence completion

Complete the following sentences to express your own opinion. Then compare your sentences with a partner.

1) In my opinion, most politicians…
2) If I were Prime Minister or President of my country I would…
3) The political system in my country is…
4) I wish politicians would…
5) In an ideal world…

Worksheet D – Politics and Youth – Reading

Read the text about Politics and Youth and put the paragraph headings in the right place.

A – **Street politics**
B – **Green generation**
C – **Parties and partying**
D - **Hi-tech politics**

Politics and Youth

Last year the BBC announced that more young people voted on Big Brother than the election. Does this make UK youth politically apathetic?

1 –

I spent a couple of days asking young people in the Manchester and London area how they felt about party politics. I spoke to 11 twenty-somethings and only one had voted in the last general election. Here's some of their comments;

'To be honest I'm not too bothered. I don't keep up with developments at Westminster [the site of UK government]. These days my job, my cash flow and socialising are more important!'
Tom, 28, from Manchester.

'I can't relate to any of the politicians. They all seem fairly similar and rarely listen to young people. Only one party [the Liberal Democrats] made student debt an issue, and they are a long way from coming to power.'
Fiona, 25, from London.
These two examples were typical of many young people's attitudes to state politics.

2 –

This would suggest that we are just not interested in politics but a closer study is more revealing.

For many young people politics is not about Westminster. Issues like the US-UK led Iraq war have sparked debate and action in recent years. In 2003 over a million people marched through London, many of them young and passionate.

3 –

Technology played a huge role in organising this protest on a global scale. It has become a factor in providing many young people across the world with a chance to interact and discuss without the traditional middle-man of the politician or news media.

The British Council's Café Society project allows young people from countries across the world to meet in a relaxed, informal setting and share opinions through video conferencing.

4 –

David Cameron, the leader of the Conservative Party, started cycling to work as gesture of the need to take green issues more seriously. Since then politicians have been keen to win the green label and secure the support of the younger generation. Young people are often perceived to be the 'greenest' age group. Indeed environmental issues are taken far more seriously than ever before. Perhaps they'll leave behind a greener UK.

SKILLS	OBJECTIVES
Integrated Skills	To identify text type To write and advice article To listen to a lecture and take notes To listen to and follow instructions To conduct a survey
Writing	To practise planning and writing texts that describe causes and effects
Reading	To read and analyse the features of texts describing cause and effect To practise timed reading
Listening	To practise listening to lectures and talks To practise listening and note taking To practise listening to texts which describe cause and effect
Speaking	Oral presentation techniques
Study Skills	To develop techniques for memorising information
Assessment	Essay – First draft due PN: Same area of study for Assessment 3: Oral presentation - to present week 9

Key references for further study

Reading activity

Selected reading

Unit 7. EAP Now! Preliminary. Kathy Cox & David Hill. 2007.

References

Module 8 Art

Module Overview

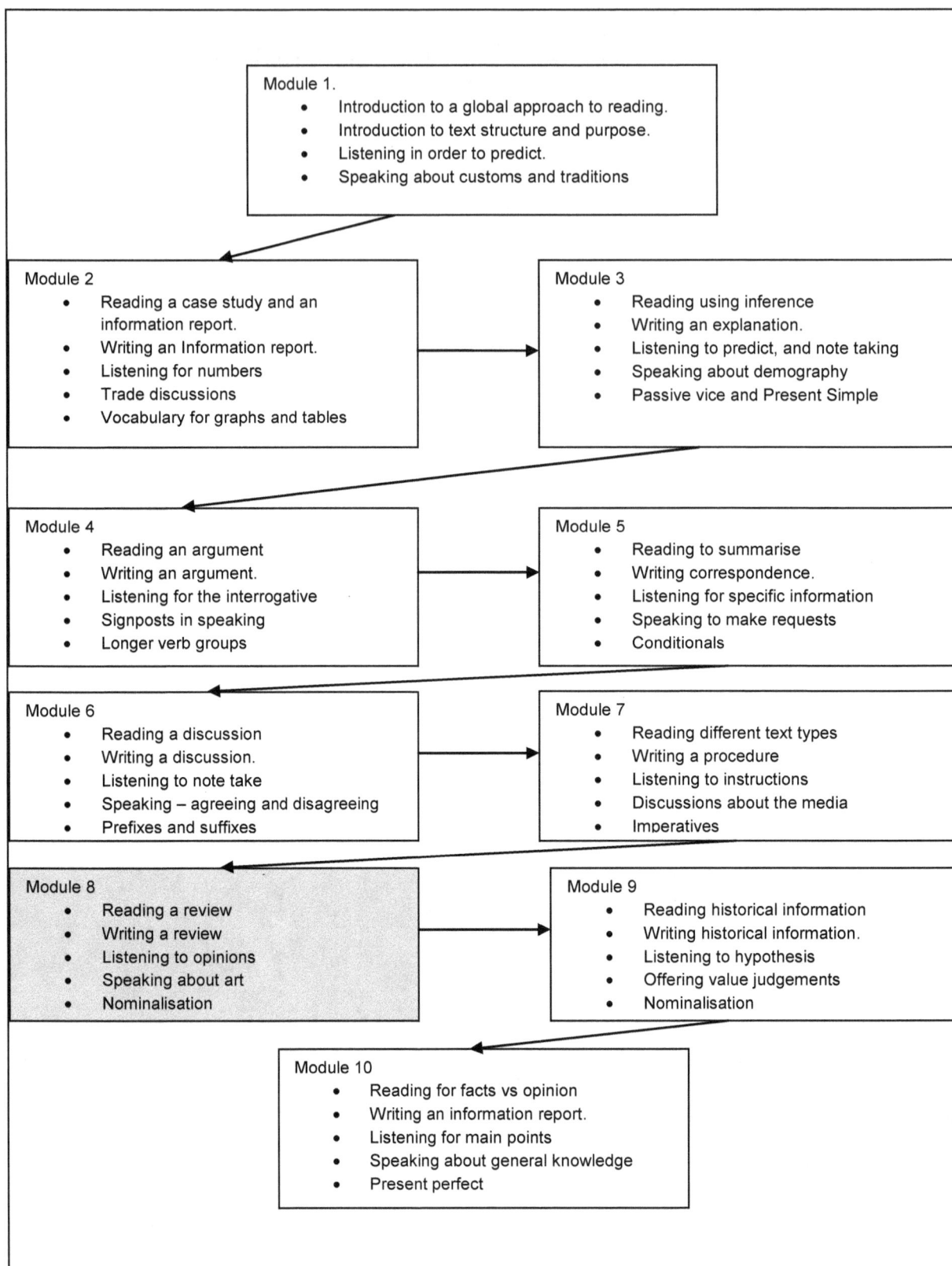

Module 1.
- Introduction to a global approach to reading.
- Introduction to text structure and purpose.
- Listening in order to predict.
- Speaking about customs and traditions

Module 2
- Reading a case study and an information report.
- Writing an Information report.
- Listening for numbers
- Trade discussions
- Vocabulary for graphs and tables

Module 3
- Reading using inference
- Writing an explanation.
- Listening to predict, and note taking
- Speaking about demography
- Passive vice and Present Simple

Module 4
- Reading an argument
- Writing an argument.
- Listening for the interrogative
- Signposts in speaking
- Longer verb groups

Module 5
- Reading to summarise
- Writing correspondence.
- Listening for specific information
- Speaking to make requests
- Conditionals

Module 6
- Reading a discussion
- Writing a discussion.
- Listening to note take
- Speaking – agreeing and disagreeing
- Prefixes and suffixes

Module 7
- Reading different text types
- Writing a procedure
- Listening to instructions
- Discussions about the media
- Imperatives

Module 8
- Reading a review
- Writing a review
- Listening to opinions
- Speaking about art
- Nominalisation

Module 9
- Reading historical information
- Writing historical information.
- Listening to hypothesis
- Offering value judgements
- Nominalisation

Module 10
- Reading for facts vs opinion
- Writing an information report.
- Listening for main points
- Speaking about general knowledge
- Present perfect

Module Objectives

Following completion of this module, you should be able to:

- Have increased their general knowledge about art and recognise that it is part of everyday life
- Have learned vocabulary including nouns and verbs, and verb tenses used in reviews
- Have improved their ability to locate definitions in context
- To be able to think critically about a subject or experience and know how to offer a review of it
- Know how to scan text for a specific purpose
- Have learned how to write a review

Learning resources

Selected Readings:

1.49: Kathy Cox. David Hill. (2004) *EAP Now! Preliminary*. Pearson Education Australia
1.50: R.R.Jordan. (2007) *New Edition Academic Writing Course*. Longman
1.51: Karen Blanchard. Christine Root. *Ready to Write More: From Paragraph to Essay*. Longman
1.52: Jack C. Richards, Samuela Eckstut-Didier. (2009) *Strategic Reading 2* Cambridge.
1.53: Helen Solorzano, Laurie Frazier. (2009) *Contemporary Topics 1-2*. Longman
1.54: Steven Gershon (2008*) Present Yourself 2: Viewpoints* Cambridge
1.55: Eric Keller, Sylvia T. Warner (2002) *Conversation Gambits* Cambridge
1.56: Michael J. Wallace. (2004) *Study Skills in English* Cambridge

Introductory comment

What do you think when you hear the word *Art*? Students will gain an understanding that art could include as many areas as painting, sculpture, ceramics, bronze casts, shadow puppets, clocks, stone lintels, maps, decorated manuscripts and so on. The concept of *Art* could have begun as many as 40,000 years BC.
Art.

Activity 1
Which of the following are NOT colours?

red   blue   green   azure   yellow   white   pink   brown   puce   rainbow   black   turquoise   navy
khaki   beige   orange   stripe   purple   violet   indigo   scarlet   magenta   grey   burgundy

Activity 2
Match the words on the left with the words on the right below to make common colour phrases.

green	tape
white	fingers
black	lie
red	card
green	jack
black	company
blue-chip	blood(ed)
blue	market

Activity 3
Write the colour phrases from Activity 2 in the spaces below then ask your partner the questions.

1. If you had a lot of money would you prefer to invest in a .... or take more of a risk?
2. Are there any .... families in your country? Do you think it is important to have aristocratic and royal families these days?
3. Is there a .... in your country? What illegal things are bought and sold on it?
4. Have you ever played ....? Would you like to? Why/not?
5. Have you ever told anyone a .... or do you always tell the truth even if you know it will upset someone?
6. Is there a lot of .... in your country or is there very little bureaucracy? What do you think should be done to reduce the amount of bureaucracy?
7. Would you like to have a .... and live and work in the USA? Why/not? What is the equivalent document in your country and how easy or difficult is it to get one?
8. Do you have .... or do plants tend to suffer under your care?

Activity 4
Read the questions below and use them to begin a conversation with your partner.

1. What colours are in fashion at the moment?
2. What are the main colours in your house or flat? Who chose them?
3. What are your favourite colours?
4. What colours suit you? What colours do you never wear? Why not?
5. What colours have special significance in your country? (For example, is white associated with weddings and black with funerals, etc?)

Activity 1

How much do you know about art? Find out in the 'true/false' quiz below.

1.	Van Gogh's first name was Victor.	T/F
2.	The statue called the Venus de Milo is in the Louvre in Paris.	T/F
3.	Pablo Picasso was a French artist.	T/F
4.	The Uffizi Gallery is in Rome, Italy.	T/F
5.	Michelangelo was a sculptor as well as a painter.	T/F
6.	Salvador Dali was a Surrealist painter.	T/F
7.	Italian painter Leonardo da Vinci died in France.	T/F
8.	American painter Jackson Pollock was an Abstract artist.	T/F

Activity 2

Read the questions and use them to start a conversation with your partner.

1. Have you got any pictures on your walls at home? If so, did you choose them? Do you like them? Why/not?
2. How important is art in your life?
3. Have you ever been to an art gallery? Did you enjoy yourself?
4. Do you think art galleries and museums should be free or should people have to pay to get in? Explain your answer.
5. Do you think children should do painting at school? Why/not?
6. Do you like abstract art or do you prefer to be able to see clearly what a painting or sculpture is of? Why?
7. Who is your favourite artist? What is your favourite painting/sculpture?

Module 8

SKILLS	OBJECTIVES
Integrated Skills	To compare and contrast texts To read for comprehension To be able to differentiate between hypothesis and fact
Writing	To practise writing comparative and contrastive texts
Reading	To practise reading and note taking To practise reading to determine the writer's point of view
Listening	To practise listening and note taking in order to follow and argument and identify a speaker's viewpoint
Speaking	Oral presentation techniques
Study Skills	To improve test taking strategies To practise techniques for writing under time pressures
Assessment	Essay – Submit Final draft

Key references for further study

Reading activity

Selected reading

Unit 8. EAP Now! Preliminary. Kathy Cox & David Hill. 2007.

References

Module 9 Architecture

Module Overview

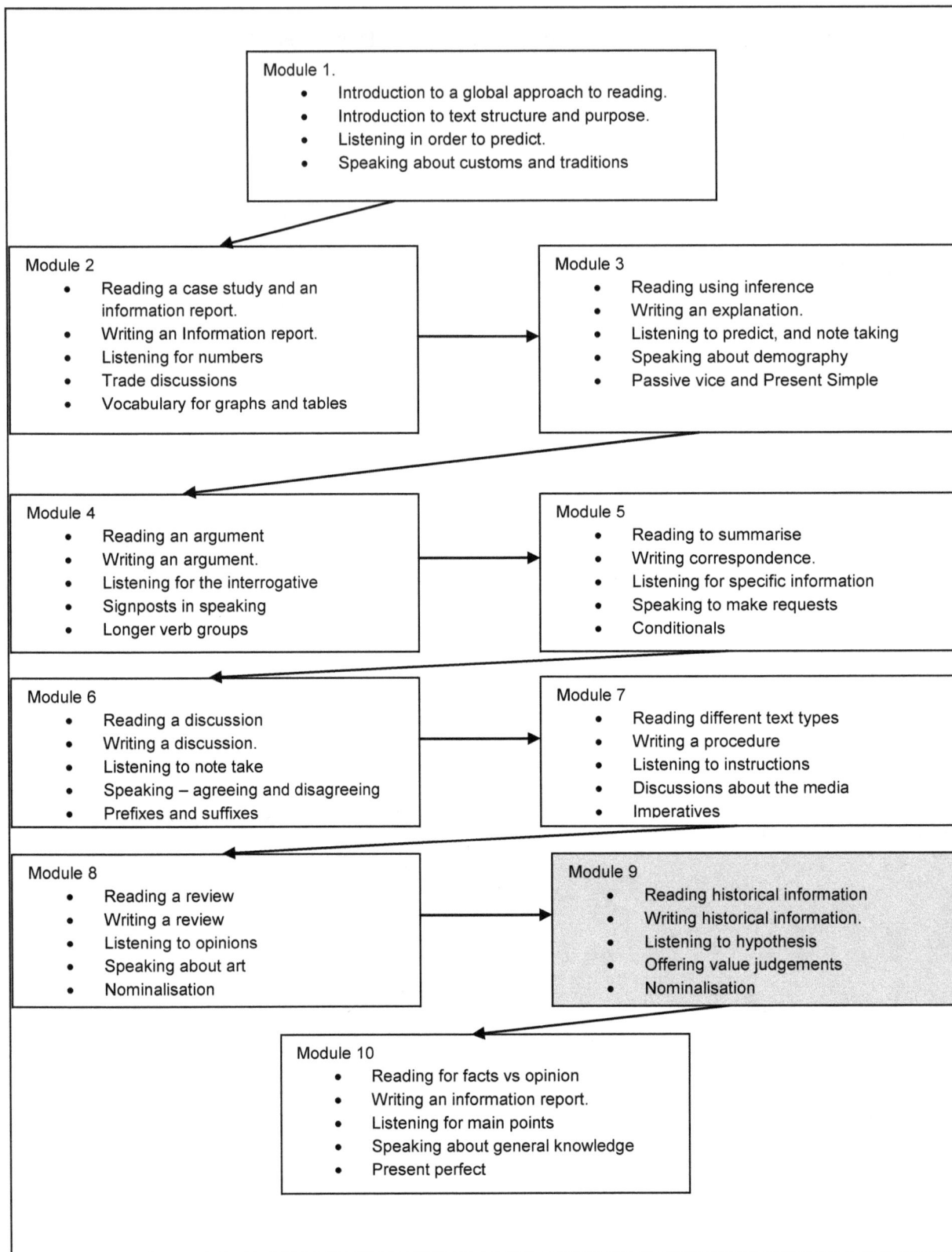

Module 1.
- Introduction to a global approach to reading.
- Introduction to text structure and purpose.
- Listening in order to predict.
- Speaking about customs and traditions

Module 2
- Reading a case study and an information report.
- Writing an Information report.
- Listening for numbers
- Trade discussions
- Vocabulary for graphs and tables

Module 3
- Reading using inference
- Writing an explanation.
- Listening to predict, and note taking
- Speaking about demography
- Passive vice and Present Simple

Module 4
- Reading an argument
- Writing an argument.
- Listening for the interrogative
- Signposts in speaking
- Longer verb groups

Module 5
- Reading to summarise
- Writing correspondence.
- Listening for specific information
- Speaking to make requests
- Conditionals

Module 6
- Reading a discussion
- Writing a discussion.
- Listening to note take
- Speaking – agreeing and disagreeing
- Prefixes and suffixes

Module 7
- Reading different text types
- Writing a procedure
- Listening to instructions
- Discussions about the media
- Imperatives

Module 8
- Reading a review
- Writing a review
- Listening to opinions
- Speaking about art
- Nominalisation

Module 9
- Reading historical information
- Writing historical information.
- Listening to hypothesis
- Offering value judgements
- Nominalisation

Module 10
- Reading for facts vs opinion
- Writing an information report.
- Listening for main points
- Speaking about general knowledge
- Present perfect

Module Objectives

Following completion of this module, you should be able to:

- ➤ Have improved their ability around comparisons in speaking and writing
- ➤ Be able to recognise and use new vocabulary related to architecture and function and form
- ➤ Have increased their general knowledge
- ➤ Have increased their understanding around ancient and classical world architecture
- ➤ Be able to recognise differences within texts in terms of more spoken writing vs academic writing
- ➤ Be able to use critical thinking to examine an important issue

Learning resources

Selected Readings:

1.57: Kathy Cox. David Hill. (2004) *EAP Now! Preliminary*. Pearson Education Australia

1.58: R.R.Jordan. (2007) *New Edition Academic Writing Course*. Longman

1.59: Karen Blanchard. Christine Root. *Ready to Write More: From Paragraph to Essay*. Longman

1.60: Jack C. Richards, Samuela Eckstut-Didier. (2009) *Strategic Reading 2* Cambridge.

1.61: Helen Solorzano, Laurie Frazier. (2009) *Contemporary Topics 1-2*. Longman

1.62: Steven Gershon (2008*) Present Yourself 2: Viewpoints* Cambridge

1.63: Eric Keller, Sylvia T. Warner (2002) *Conversation Gambits* Cambridge

1.64: Michael J. Wallace. (2004) *Study Skills in English* Cambridge

Introductory comment

Building in hot latitudes presents its own particular challenges, but even the most extreme climates can give rise to intuitive forms of architecture that have an important role to play in the search for a new ecological responsiveness.
Architecture.

Name

Survey your local area to find examples of ancient Greek architectural styles.

Put a tick for every time you see a design similar to those on this sheet.

The development of pillar styles

pediment

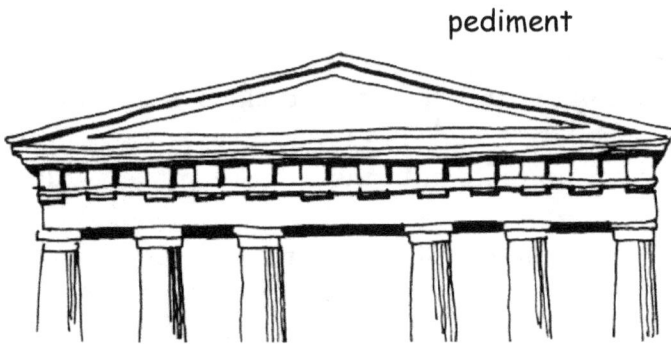

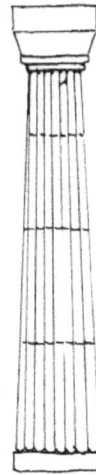  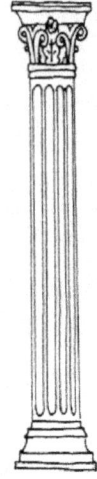

doric ionic corinthia

tick

tick	tick	tick

egg and tongue pattern

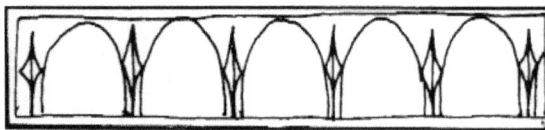

t	
i	
^	

swirl pattern

t	
i	
^	

key pattern

t	
i	
^	

Advanced architecture vocabulary

Read the lists of vocabulary below and guess what kind of building each list is related to:

Steeple
Altar
Gargoyles
Chapel
Sculpture
Lobby
Balconies
Indoor pool
Tearoom
Aisle
Store room/ warehouse
Cash machine (= ATM)
Safe
Detached
Terraced
Back garden
Loft
Pond
Chimney pot
Brick
Doorstep
Mock Tudor
Eaves
Moat
Drawbridge
Well
Jousting ground
Platforms
Ticket office
Balcony
Lobby
The gods
A and E (= ER)
In patients
X ray room
Playground
Cafeteria
State rooms
Chandelier
Guard house
Fountain
Courtyard
Fireplace
Cellar
Beer garden
Reinforced concrete
Balcony
Helicopter landing pad
Lift (= elevator)
The stands
Press box
Dome
(Artificial) turf
Minaret
Cafeteria
Executive floor
Smoking area

Stained glass windows
Aisle
Belfry
Confession box
Font
Ballroom
Chandelier
Bar

Till (= checkout = register)
Deli counter
Security cameras
Reinforced glass
Semi-detached
Front garden
Fence
Cellar
Chimney
Thatch
Double glazing
Lawn
Greenhouse
Patio
Arrow slits
Keep
Stables

Ticket barrier

Stage
Ticket office
The orchestra pit
Waiting room
Out patients

Reception
Gym
Throne room
Sentry box
Stables
Statue
Parade ground
Lounge
Bar

Plate glass windows
Studio flats
Penthouse

Ticket office
Corporate hospitality suites
Retractable roof
Changing rooms
Prayer hall
Skyscraper
Executive elevator

Use vocabulary like that above to design/ describe a new iconic building for the city where you live, e.g. a cathedral that is also a skyscraper.

Activity 1

With your partner make a list of all the things you can find in a bathroom.

....
....
....
....

Activity 2

Decide which of the following words are NOT euphemisms for 'the toilet' in British English.

**the little boy's/girl's room   the powder room   the box
the smallest room   the cloakroom
the throne   the loo   the lavatory   the ladies'
the seat   the gents'   the bathroom
the washroom   the bog   the john**

Activity 3

Decide if the following statements are true or false.

1. 2.6 billion people in the world have no toilet at home.
2. Nearly 40% of the world's population lack access to a proper toilet.
3. Over 60% of people in Africa do not have access to a proper toilet.
4. Over 100 million people in Latin America do not have a toilet.
5. 2009 will be the 'International Year of Sanitation'.

Activity 4

Use the following questions to start a conversation with your partner.

1. State-of-the-art loos can greet you, play music, massage your buttocks with sprays of water and collect samples of your urine for analysis – the information being sent to a doctor on the Internet via a mobile phone device installed in the toilet. What are the advantages and disadvantages of technological features like this being included in toilets?
2. What other devices would you like to have installed in future loos?
3. What are the main differences between toilets in your country and those in other countries?
4. How do you think public conveniences could be improved?
5. Should people have to pay to use a public convenience or should it be free?
6. What do you think the penalty should be for urinating in public?
7. What are the main advantages and disadvantages of squat toilets?
8. Do you think having access to a real toilet is a basic human right?
9. Imagine a world without loos. How would life be different without toilets?
10. Have you ever dropped anything you value (e.g. a ring) down the toilet? What did you do?

Module 9

SKILLS	OBJECTIVES
Integrated Skills	To compare and contrast tests To propose solutions To write a solution To comprehend meaning in context and recognise facts
Writing	To practise writing comparative and contrastive texts
Reading	To practise reading and note taking To practise reading to determine the writer's point of view
Listening	To practise listening and note taking in order to follow and argument and identify a speaker's viewpoint
Speaking	
Study Skills	To improve test taking strategies To practise techniques for writing under time pressures
Assessment	Oral Presentation

Key references for further study

Reading activity

Selected reading

Unit 9. EAP Now! Preliminary. Kathy Cox & David Hill. 2007.

References

Module 10 Indigenous People

Module Overview

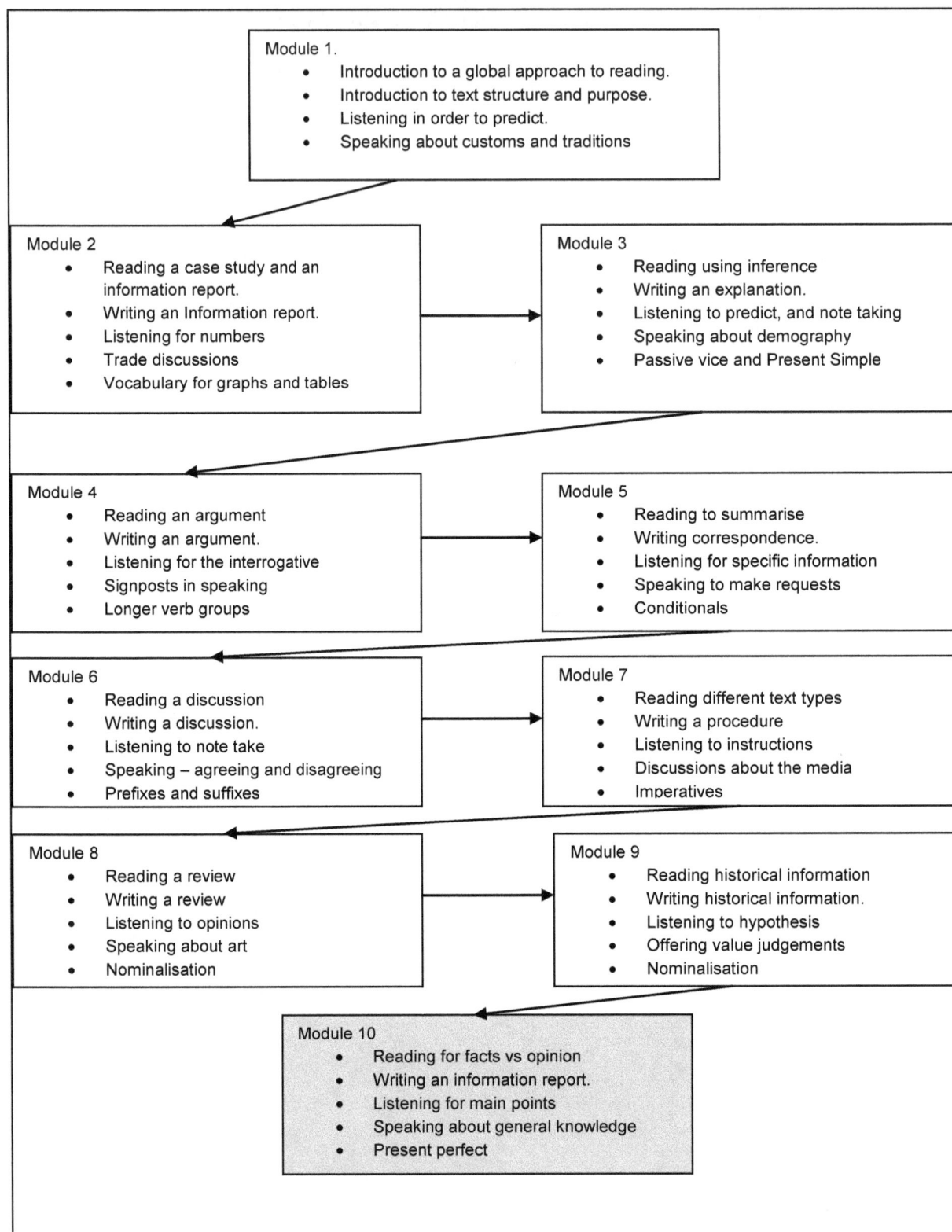

Module 1.
- Introduction to a global approach to reading.
- Introduction to text structure and purpose.
- Listening in order to predict.
- Speaking about customs and traditions

Module 2
- Reading a case study and an information report.
- Writing an Information report.
- Listening for numbers
- Trade discussions
- Vocabulary for graphs and tables

Module 3
- Reading using inference
- Writing an explanation.
- Listening to predict, and note taking
- Speaking about demography
- Passive vice and Present Simple

Module 4
- Reading an argument
- Writing an argument.
- Listening for the interrogative
- Signposts in speaking
- Longer verb groups

Module 5
- Reading to summarise
- Writing correspondence.
- Listening for specific information
- Speaking to make requests
- Conditionals

Module 6
- Reading a discussion
- Writing a discussion.
- Listening to note take
- Speaking – agreeing and disagreeing
- Prefixes and suffixes

Module 7
- Reading different text types
- Writing a procedure
- Listening to instructions
- Discussions about the media
- Imperatives

Module 8
- Reading a review
- Writing a review
- Listening to opinions
- Speaking about art
- Nominalisation

Module 9
- Reading historical information
- Writing historical information.
- Listening to hypothesis
- Offering value judgements
- Nominalisation

Module 10
- Reading for facts vs opinion
- Writing an information report.
- Listening for main points
- Speaking about general knowledge
- Present perfect

Module Objectives

Following completion of this module, you should be able to:

- ➢ How to relate to the theme in a personalised way
- ➢ Have found opportunities to learn and practise vocabulary and ways of expressing ideas
- ➢ Have practised reading texts for ideas expressed as fact
- ➢ Have practised writing a report
- ➢ Have consolidated how to use present perfect continuous
- ➢ Know how to identify a text and match it with its source

Learning resources

Selected Readings:

1.65: Kathy Cox. David Hill. (2004) *EAP Now! Preliminary*. Pearson Education Australia
1.66: R.R.Jordan. (2007) *New Edition Academic Writing Course*. Longman
1.67: Karen Blanchard. Christine Root. *Ready to Write More: From Paragraph to Essay*. Longman
1.68: Jack C. Richards, Samuela Eckstut-Didier. (2009) *Strategic Reading 2* Cambridge.
1.69: Helen Solorzano, Laurie Frazier. (2009) *Contemporary Topics 1-2*. Longman
1.70: Steven Gershon (2008) *Present Yourself 2: Viewpoints* Cambridge
1.71: Eric Keller, Sylvia T. Warner (2002) *Conversation Gambits* Cambridge
1.72: Michael J. Wallace. (2004) *Study Skills in English* Cambridge

Introductory comment

A traditional group is a number of persons formed together due to their gender, nationality, religion and traditions. In Australian society an example of a traditional group is Aboriginals.
Indigenous People.

1. What's it like to be a refugee?

The following activities will help students to:

- identify reasons why people become refugees
- explore the circumstances in which refugees flee their homes
- encourage empathy with refugees
- promote understanding of the spontaneous exodus experienced by many fleeing their home countries
- encourage students to empathise with their flight
- foster debate about priorities in a survival situation.

Step 1

Using the activity sheet *What's it like to be a refugee?*, students are encouraged to explore the meaning of the words 'refugee' and 'asylum seeker' and brainstorm the reasons why people might seek asylum and become refugees. A follow up discussion is useful here to assist students in developing an understanding of the concepts 'refugee' and 'asylum seeker'. Key questions to break down the definitions provided in *Face the Facts* could include:

Q1: Are refugees the same as migrants?

Encourage students to explore this question by looking at push and pull factors that cause people to migrate. Push factors may cause people to leave their homelands while pull factors attract people to new countries. Explain that the push factors are more important for refugees than for migrants.

Q2: Are refugees all people who flee from dangerous situations?

Assist students in understanding that while there are many reasons people may be forced to leave their homeland (for example war, or environmental disasters like floods or earthquakes), refugees are fleeing because of a well-founded fear of specific kinds of persecution related to their: race, religion, nationality, membership of a particular social group or political opinion.

Teachers may wish to explore difficult terms like 'well-founded fear' (i.e. there has to be a real chance of being persecuted) or 'persecution' (ie a serious punishment or some significant disadvantage inflicted by a government or by individuals or a group that the government cannot or will not control). Teachers may also wish to explore in more detail the reasons for fleeing persecution by providing specific individual or group examples. For example:

Race:	Albert Einstein fleeing Nazi Germany in 1933.
Religion:	The Dalai Lama fleeing Tibet after the Chinese take-over in 1950.
Nationality:	Bosnian refugees from the former Yugoslavia Membership of a particular social group/ Tamils fleeing Sri Lanka after 1948.
Political opinion:	Lenin fleeing Tsarist Russia in 1900.

Q3: Who decides who is a refugee?

Refer to *Face the Facts Question 3.1 – who are asylum seekers?* and explore the concept of asylum pointing out:

- refugees seek asylum outside their country of usual residence or origin
- governments of individual countries and organisations like the United Nations High Commissioner for Refugees determine who is a refugee
- everyone has a right to seek asylum from persecution – this is a fundamental human right set out in the Universal Declaration of Human Rights (Article 14)

- no country can forcibly return refugees to a territory where they face persecution – this is set out in Article 33 of the United Nations Convention and Protocol Relating to the Status of Refugees and is known as the principle of 'non-refoulement'.

Seeking refuge – what will you take with you?

1. You have half an hour before you must leave your home. Work out the list of things that you would like to take with you. All members of your group must agree about what's on the list.

2. You are allowed to take one small suitcase with you. You cannot take anything that doesn't fit. You cannot take anything that has to be carried separately. You cannot ask family members to carry anything for you. Revise the list of things so that it will fit in your suitcase. Everyone in your group must agree about what's on the list.

3. After you have finalised your list, identify ONE item you would keep if you had to leave all else behind.

4. After your group has finalised your list, report back to the class on the situation you imagined which forced you to become a refugee and explain the items you have included on your list and why.

What's it like to be a refugee?

1. Working individually, read *Face the Facts – Questions and Answers about Refugees and Asylum Seekers* to gather the facts about refugees and asylum seekers. After you have finished reading, answer the questions below.

a. What is a refugee?

....

....

b. What is an asylum seeker?

....

....

Discuss your answers with your classmates.

2. Create the story of an imaginary family of asylum seekers (compare the information you have gathered above) using the questions in the text box below.

a. Why are they fleeing?

....

....

....

b. How many family members are there? ....

c. What is their country of origin? ....

d. Other relevant information?

....

....

....

....

You may wish to explore real-life personal stories of asylum seekers to help you to create your imaginary family. Useful information is available at:

Road to Refuge
Developed by the BBC, this site explores the stories of refugees from around the world, using first-person testimonies and in-depth interviews. http://news.bbc.co.uk/hi/english/static/in_depth/world/2001/road_to_refuge/

Scattered People
Developed through a partnership between Lifeline Brisbane, the Refugee Claimants Support Centre, and Brisbane City Council, this site includes the stories of refugee claimants and their response to seeking asylum in Australia. http://brisbane-stories.powerup.com.au/scatteredpeople/

Use *Face the Facts – Questions and Answers about Asylum Seekers and Refugees*, as a starting point for your research and explore the real-life stories of asylum seekers to gather ideas for your story.

3a. Imagine that you (and your group) are one of the family members seeking asylum in another country (parents, children, grandparents etc). What would you take with you?

Seeking refuge – what will you take with you?

You have half an hour before you must leave your home.

Work out the list of things that you would like to take with you. Think carefully about the items you include on your list:

- what will you need to survive the journey?
- what will you need when you arrive?
- what personal items will you take with you?

....

....

....

....

....

....

....

....

....

....

You are allowed to take one small suitcase with you. You cannot take anything that doesn't fit. You cannot take anything that has to be carried separately. You cannot ask family members to carry anything for you. Revise the list of things so that they will fit in your suitcase. Everyone in your group must agree about what's on the list.

After you have finalised your list, identify ONE item you would keep if you had to leave all else behind.

....

Explain why this item is important.

....

....

....

....

....

3b. After your group has finalised your list, report back to the class on the situation which forced you to become a refugee and explain the items you have included in your suitcase and why.

4. Using the lists your group has created and the scenario you imagined at the beginning of the activity, work individually to create a more detailed story about your refugee family.

You could present it as a:

- written testimony
- an imaginary diary of your refugee's journey to Australia
- artwork
- an audio recording of your refugee's story.

Notes

....

....

....

....

....

....

....

....

....

....

....

SKILLS	OBJECTIVES
Integrated Skills	To be able to skim and scan texts effectively To take notes from texts To be able to match genres to tasks To listen for specific information
Writing	To review the use of connectives in texts To consolidate self-editing skills
Reading	To apply reading strategies to longer texts
Listening	To practise listening and note taking To identify main points, key words and factual/non-factual information in extended talks To apply note-taking skills in a lecture
Speaking	Review oral presentations
Study Skills	To improve test taking strategies To practise techniques for writing under time pressures
Tests	Listening, Reading and Writing tests

Key references for further study

Reading activity

Selected reading

Unit 10. EAP Now! Preliminary. Kathy Cox & David Hill. 2007.

References

Module 11 Landscapes

Module Overview (Extension)

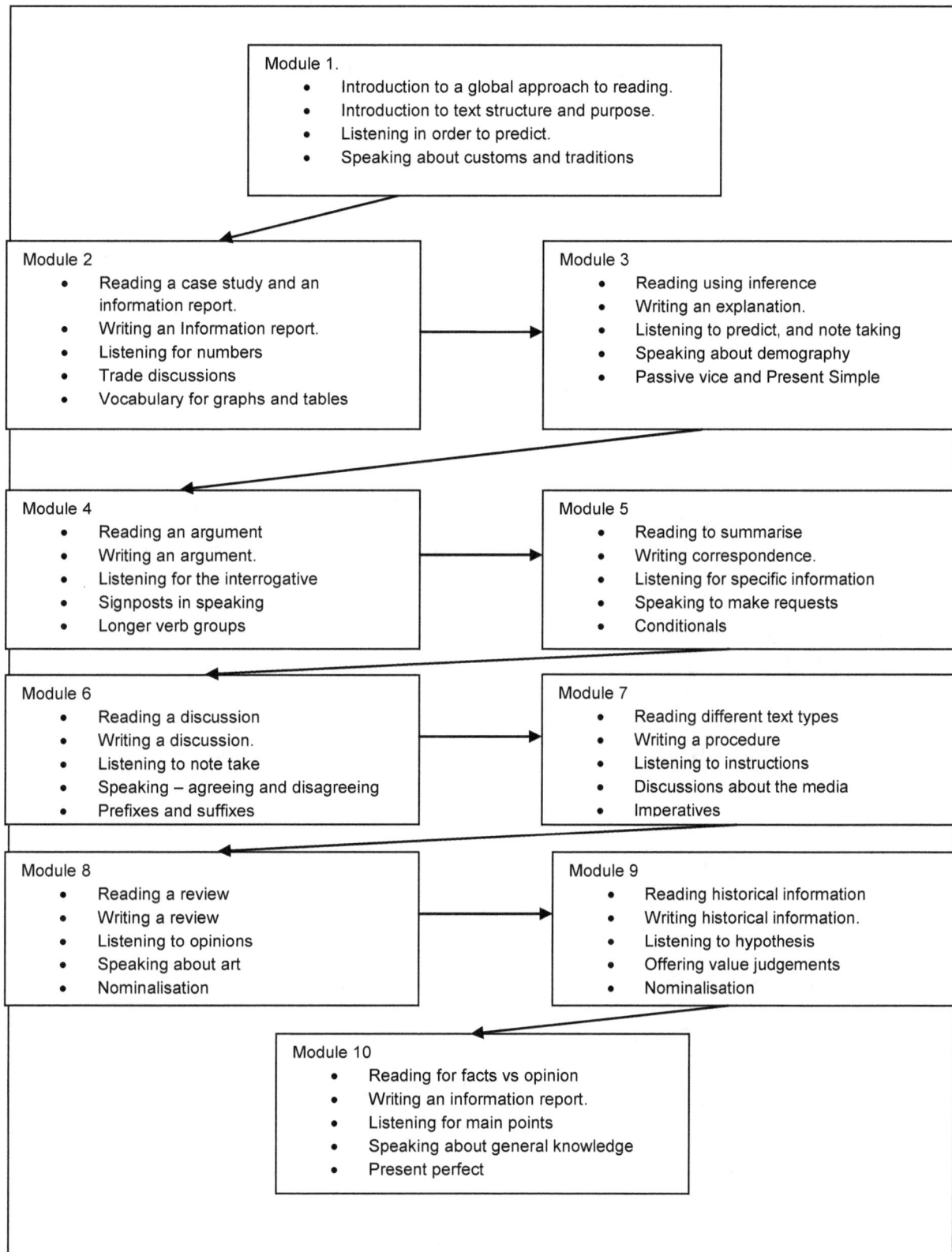

Module 1.
- Introduction to a global approach to reading.
- Introduction to text structure and purpose.
- Listening in order to predict.
- Speaking about customs and traditions

Module 2
- Reading a case study and an information report.
- Writing an Information report.
- Listening for numbers
- Trade discussions
- Vocabulary for graphs and tables

Module 3
- Reading using inference
- Writing an explanation.
- Listening to predict, and note taking
- Speaking about demography
- Passive vice and Present Simple

Module 4
- Reading an argument
- Writing an argument.
- Listening for the interrogative
- Signposts in speaking
- Longer verb groups

Module 5
- Reading to summarise
- Writing correspondence.
- Listening for specific information
- Speaking to make requests
- Conditionals

Module 6
- Reading a discussion
- Writing a discussion.
- Listening to note take
- Speaking – agreeing and disagreeing
- Prefixes and suffixes

Module 7
- Reading different text types
- Writing a procedure
- Listening to instructions
- Discussions about the media
- Imperatives

Module 8
- Reading a review
- Writing a review
- Listening to opinions
- Speaking about art
- Nominalisation

Module 9
- Reading historical information
- Writing historical information.
- Listening to hypothesis
- Offering value judgements
- Nominalisation

Module 10
- Reading for facts vs opinion
- Writing an information report.
- Listening for main points
- Speaking about general knowledge
- Present perfect

Module Objectives

Following completion of this module, you should be able to:

> ➢ Understand different interpretations of the landscape theme
> ➢ Know how to interpret an aerial map in order to increase vocabulary
> ➢ Be able to apply learned knowledge in a different task
> ➢ Be able to propose solutions using key words
> ➢ Be able to locate key words for explanations within a text
> ➢ Be able to discuss geographic features of landscapes in order to increase general knowledge

Learning resources

Selected Readings:

1.73: Kathy Cox. David Hill. (2004) *EAP Now! Preliminary*. Pearson Education Australia

1.74: R.R.Jordan. (2007) *New Edition Academic Writing Course*. Longman

1.75: Karen Blanchard. Christine Root. *Ready to Write More: From Paragraph to Essay*. Longman

1.76: Jack C. Richards, Samuela Eckstut-Didier. (2009) *Strategic Reading 2* Cambridge.

1.77: Helen Solorzano, Laurie Frazier. (2009) *Contemporary Topics 1-2*. Longman

1.78: Steven Gershon (2008*) Present Yourself 2: Viewpoints* Cambridge

1.79: Eric Keller, Sylvia T. Warner (2002) *Conversation Gambits* Cambridge

1.80: Michael J. Wallace. (2004) *Study Skills in English* Cambridge

Introductory comment

From Wikipedia, the free encyclopedia

Landscape comprises the visible features of an area of land, including the physical elements of landforms, water bodies such as rivers, lakes and the sea, living elements of land cover including indigenous vegetation, human elements including land uses, buildings and structures, and transitory elements such as lighting and weather conditions.

.

Landscapes.

Geography Word Search

Complete the activity.

```
L  D  T  C  V  X  Y  B  L  V  C  F  H  N  N
T  Q  S  J  P  E  N  I  N  S  U  L  A  C  D
B  A  J  A  L  D  M  P  Q  I  P  W  F  O  H
L  C  Y  F  C  K  C  L  I  S  T  H  M  U  S
A  Y  O  I  R  H  H  A  Z  E  L  A  J  A  N
K  G  Q  C  W  H  G  T  P  D  L  K  R  P  B
E  X  M  M  A  J  O  E  G  H  W  C  Q  P  T
L  F  G  X  V  P  G  A  X  Y  H  T  T  X  Q
S  Y  O  U  B  G  E  U  I  I  S  D  L  H  M
X  T  A  J  L  A  D  N  P  S  Y  V  O  Q  D
L  H  R  X  G  F  Y  E  J  R  I  O  H  W  I
C  G  P  A  L  Z  L  F  E  Q  W  N  M  C  P
A  G  K  E  I  A  Y  S  P  Z  L  L  V  H  G
L  Y  S  L  G  T  J  I  S  L  A  N  D  V  O
U  D  J  O  Q  X  X  A  A  A  Z  S  O  Y  E
```

strait	lake	bay	peninsula
plateau	gulf	cape	
island	archipelago	isthmus	

Geography Vocabulary

Complete the activity.

1. _____ Land surrounded on 3 sides by water

2. _____ large group of islands

3. _____ A narrow strip of land connecting two larger forms

4. _____ A narrow passageway connecting two large bodies of water

5. _____ A portion of an ocean or sea extending into the land; a partially land-locked sea

6. _____ A small body of water set off from the main body

7. _____ A large body of water surrounded by land

8. _____ Piece of land extending into a large body of water

9. _____ An area of elevated flat land

10. _____ Land surrounded on all sides by water, smaller than a continent

island	bay	lake
archipelago	gulf	isthmus
plateau	peninsula	
cape	strait	

Geography Crossword Puzzle

Complete the activity.

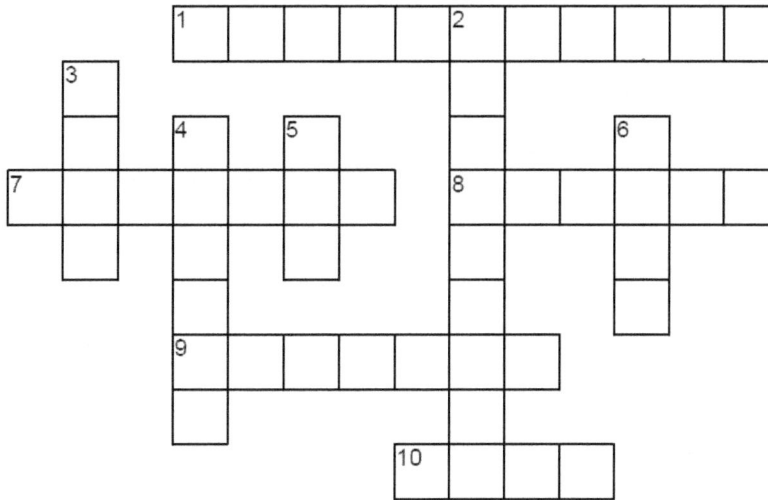

```
        ┌─┬─┬─┬─┬─┬─┬─┬─┬─┬─┐
        │1│ │ │ │ │2│ │ │ │ │
   ┌─┐  └─┴─┴─┴─┴─┼─┼─┴─┴─┴─┘
   │3│            │ │
   ├─┼─┬─┐  ┌─┐   │ │        ┌─┐
   │ │4│ │  │5│   │ │        │6│
┌─┬┼─┼─┼─┼──┼─┼───┼─┼────────┼─┤
│7│ │ │ │   │ │   │8│ │ │ │ │ │ │
└─┴┼─┴─┼─┘  │ │   │ │        │ │
   │   │    │ │   │ │        │ │
   │   │  ┌─┼─┼───┼─┼─┬─┐    │ │
   │   │  │9│ │   │ │ │ │    │ │
   │   │  └─┼─┼───┴─┴─┴─┘    └─┘
   │   │    │ │
          ┌─┼─┼─┬─┐
          │10 │ │ │
          └───┴─┴─┘
```

ACROSS

1. large group of islands
7. An area of elevated flat land
8. Land surrounded on all sides by water, smaller than a continent
9. A narrow strip of land connecting two larger forms
10. A large body of water surrounded by land

DOWN

2. Land surrounded on 3 sides by water
3. A portion of an ocean or sea extending into the land; a partially land-locked sea
4. A narrow passageway connecting two large bodies of water
5. A small body of water set off from the main body
6. Piece of land extending into a large body of water

peninsula	bay	cape
strait	plateau	archipelago
isthmus	island	
gulf	lake	

Put the words in alphabetical order

Name: _____

Date: _____

Geography Alphabet Activity

Complete the activity.

1. _____

2. _____

3. _____

4. _____

5. _____

6. _____

7. _____

8. _____

9. _____

10. _____

gulf	bay	peninsula
cape	plateau	isthmus
lake	island	
archipelago	strait	

Name: _____

Date: _____

Geography Challenge

Complete the activity.

___1. A portion of an ocean or sea extending into the land; a partially land-locked sea
    A. strait   B. plateau   C. gulf   D. archipelago

___2. A small body of water set off from the main body
    A. peninsula   B. lake   C. bay   D. archipelago

___3. Land surrounded on all sides by water, smaller than a continent
    A. plateau   B. strait   C. island   D. isthmus

___4. A large body of water surrounded by land
    A. strait   B. peninsula   C. lake   D. cape

___5. Land surrounded on 3 sides by water
    A. lake   B. plateau   C. isthmus   D. peninsula

___6. A narrow strip of land connecting two larger forms
    A. bay   B. strait   C. isthmus   D. plateau

___7. An area of elevated flat land
    A. peninsula   B. archipelago   C. cape   D. plateau

___8. Piece of land extending into a large body of water
    A. plateau   B. archipelago   C. gulf   D. cape

___9. large group of islands
    A. cape   B. isthmus   C. strait   D. archipelago

___10. A narrow passageway connecting two large bodies of water
    A. lake   B. cape   C. bay   D. strait

Peninsula

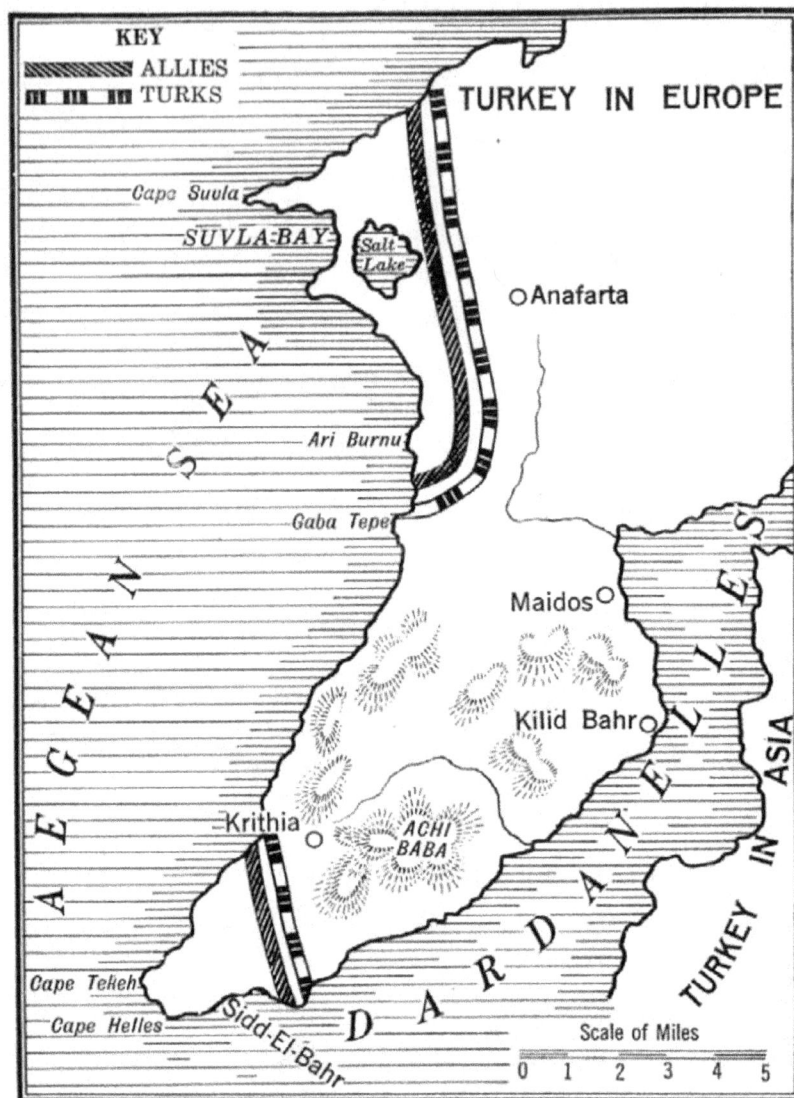

Definition: _____

_____

_____

Module 11

SKILLS	OBJECTIVES
Integrated Skills	To be able to skim and scan texts effectively To take notes from texts To be able to match genres to tasks To listen for specific information
Writing	To review the use of connectives in texts To consolidate self-editing skills
Reading	To apply reading strategies to longer texts
Listening	To practise listening and note taking To identify main points, key words and factual/non-factual information in extended talks To apply note-taking skills in a lecture
Speaking	Review oral presentations
Study Skills	To improve test taking strategies To practise techniques for writing under time pressures
Tests	Listening, Reading and Writing tests

Key references for further study

Reading activity

Selected reading

Unit 11. EAP Now! Preliminary. Kathy Cox & David Hill. 2007.

References

Module 12 Landscapes

Module Overview (Extension)

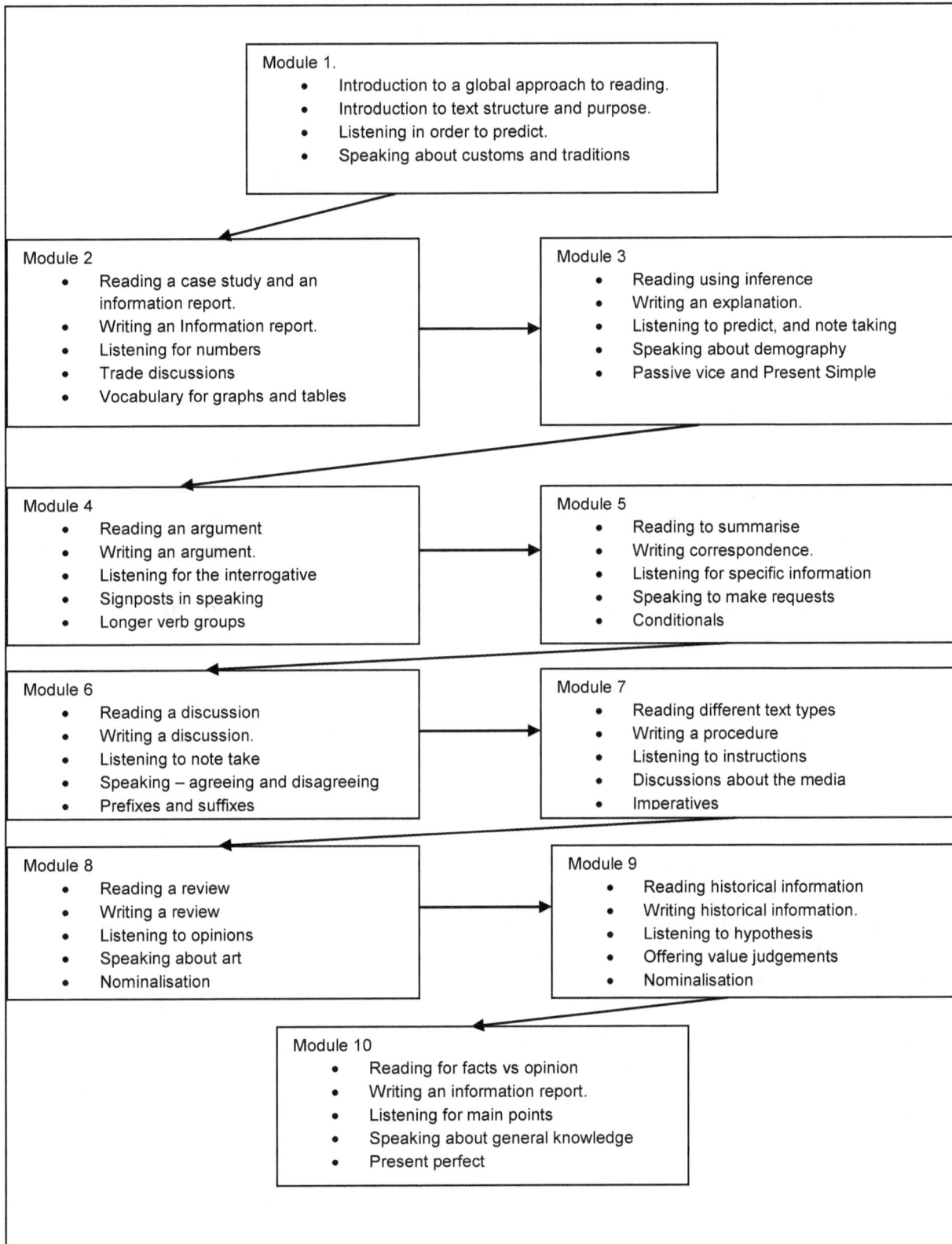

Module 1.
- Introduction to a global approach to reading.
- Introduction to text structure and purpose.
- Listening in order to predict.
- Speaking about customs and traditions

Module 2
- Reading a case study and an information report.
- Writing an Information report.
- Listening for numbers
- Trade discussions
- Vocabulary for graphs and tables

Module 3
- Reading using inference
- Writing an explanation.
- Listening to predict, and note taking
- Speaking about demography
- Passive vice and Present Simple

Module 4
- Reading an argument
- Writing an argument.
- Listening for the interrogative
- Signposts in speaking
- Longer verb groups

Module 5
- Reading to summarise
- Writing correspondence.
- Listening for specific information
- Speaking to make requests
- Conditionals

Module 6
- Reading a discussion
- Writing a discussion.
- Listening to note take
- Speaking – agreeing and disagreeing
- Prefixes and suffixes

Module 7
- Reading different text types
- Writing a procedure
- Listening to instructions
- Discussions about the media
- Imperatives

Module 8
- Reading a review
- Writing a review
- Listening to opinions
- Speaking about art
- Nominalisation

Module 9
- Reading historical information
- Writing historical information.
- Listening to hypothesis
- Offering value judgements
- Nominalisation

Module 10
- Reading for facts vs opinion
- Writing an information report.
- Listening for main points
- Speaking about general knowledge
- Present perfect

Module Objectives

Following completion of this module, you should be able to:

- Be able to talk about various world topics more fluently
- Have reviewed the essay genres that they may have to write at college or university
- Have seen connections between essay questions and the genre of the answer
- Have practised writing an opinion essay using at least one essay genre
- Have practised listening for specific information
- Have practised the speaking skills required in a tutorial

Learning resources

Selected Readings:

- 1.81: Kathy Cox. David Hill. (2004) *EAP Now! Preliminary*. Pearson Education Australia
- 1.82: R.R.Jordan. (2007) *New Edition Academic Writing Course*. Longman
- 1.83: Karen Blanchard. Christine Root. *Ready to Write More: From Paragraph to Essay*. Longman
- 1.84: Jack C. Richards, Samuela Eckstut-Didier. (2009) *Strategic Reading 2* Cambridge.
- 1.85: Helen Solorzano, Laurie Frazier. (2009) *Contemporary Topics 1-2*. Longman
- 1.86: Steven Gershon (2008*) Present Yourself 2: Viewpoints* Cambridge
- 1.87: Eric Keller, Sylvia T. Warner (2002) *Conversation Gambits* Cambridge
- 1.88: Michael J. Wallace. (2004) *Study Skills in English* Cambridge

Introductory comment

Globalization (or **globalisation**) describes the process by which regional economies, societies, and cultures have become integrated through a global network of political ideas through communication, transportation, and trade. The term is most closely associated with the term economic globalization: the integration of national economies into the international economy through trade,foreign direct investment, capital flows, migration, the spread of technology, and military presence.[1] However, globalization is usually recognized as being driven by a combination of economic, technological, sociocultural, political, and biological factors.[2] The term can also refer to the transnational circulation of ideas, languages, or popular culture through acculturation. An aspect of the world which has gone through the process can be said to be **globalized**.

World

Module 12

SKILLS	OBJECTIVES
Integrated Skills	To be able to skim and scan texts effectively To take notes from texts To be able to match genres to tasks To listen for specific information
Writing	To review the use of connectives in texts To consolidate self-editing skills
Reading	To apply reading strategies to longer texts
Listening	To practise listening and note taking To identify main points, key words and factual/non-factual information in extended talks To apply note-taking skills in a lecture
Speaking	Review oral presentations
Study Skills	To improve test taking strategies To practise techniques for writing under time pressures
Tests	Listening, Reading and Writing tests

Name_____

What's New?

From what source did you get most of your information? (radio, TV, internet, newspaper)
_____

Write the <u>main idea</u> for each of the following types of news stories from this week. REMEMBER, this is not a headline, but the main idea of the news article.

World News Item _____

National News Item _____

Local News Item _____

Sports News Item _____

Choose one of the stories from above and list the 5 Ws.

<u>Who</u> was the story about? _____

<u>What</u> happened? _____

<u>Where</u> did it happen? _____

<u>When</u> did it happen? _____

<u>Why</u> did it happen? (the cause)

_____

From this week's news, make up a trivia question that you think may stump the class.

News Article Analysis Worksheet

Newspaper: _____ Date: _____

Name of article: _____

The 5 "W's" and "H"

1. Who? _____

2. What? _____

3. Where? _____

4. When? _____

5. Why? _____

6. How? _____

Were all the 5 "W's" and "H" answered?

Of all the 5 "W's" and "H", star the one you think is the most important. Tell why.

Is the story international, national or local?

What do you think of this article? (Give at least three sentences)

CURRENT EVENTS WORKSHEET

Title of Article:_____

WHO is this article about? :_____

WHAT is this story about? List four facts and/or opinions related in your article and identify them as facts or opinions.

1.

2.

3.

4.

WHEN did this story take place? _____

WHERE is this event or issue occurring?   (Specify city, country, region, etc.)

_____

HOW is this story important? _____

_____

PREDICT what you think might happen as this story develops.

1. Proper Heading (3 Points)

Name: _____   Date: _____

Teacher: _____   Period: _____

Current Events

2. Title of Article *(3 points)*: _____

3. Source of article *(3 points)*: _____

4. Author of article *(3 points)*: _____

5. Date of article *(3 points)*: _____

6. Exact location: Latitude*(3 points)*: _____   Longitude*(3 points)*: _____

City *(3 points)*: _____ Continent*(3 points)*: _____ Country*(3 points)*: _____

7. 3-5 Vocabulary words with Definitions that are appropriate to the article *(15 points)*:

    1.

    2.

    3.

    4.

    5.

8. Short Paragraph (3-5 sentences that tells how this article relates to what we are learning in class) *(10 points)*:

9. Long paragraph (8+ sentences that summarizes the article in *your own words*) *(25 points)*:

Article summaries must be TYPED, using BLACK ink, and should be 1.5 LINE SPACING

Joan Smith   9-16-03
Miss Hill   Social Studies

-OR-

Joan Smith   9-16-03
Mr. McGee   Science

Title of article: "Too much rain hits the Northeast"

Source: New York Times

Author: Jeff Doe

Date: 9-10-04

Exact Location: 76° N, 93° W, New York, North America, USA

3-5 Vocabulary words:

    1. Torrential: An abundance of something, usually refers to water

    2. Inundated: to cover with or as if with a flood

    3. Humidity: the amount of atmospheric moisture

    4. Flood: to fill abundantly or excessively

    5. Water table: the upper limit of the portion of the ground wholly saturated with water

Short Paragraph:

    In Social Studies (or Science) we are learning about climates and climate zones. This article writes about climates and how in the northeast there is too much rain falling. The land is flooding and that does not happen in all climate zones, as we are learning in class.

Long Paragraph:

    The article writes about flooding in the northeast. There is too much rain and the land is inundated. According to one expert, "The water table in many areas is much higher than it has been in past years." This means good things for the farmers. It is a bad thing because the water has no where to go and the roads get flooded. Some houses were washed away in the floods. According to an eye-witness during the last storm, "People were not driving through the streets, they were in boats, paddling their way to other houses." While rain is usually good for the land, this rain needs to stop so that the ground can absorb the water that has already fallen and people can "get their lives back in order." This article was informational in that it described what can happen to people and the land when there is too much rain.

Key references for further study

Reading activity

Selected reading

Unit 12. EAP Now! Preliminary. Kathy Cox & David Hill. 2007.

References

EAP Assessment

Due	Tasks	Assessment	Weighting
Week 4 First draft due Week 5 Final draft due	Compile a report, in appropriate genre and format, describing a process	500 word report	10%
Week 5 Tests	Listening Reading Writing	Test	10% 10% 5%
Week 7 First draft due Week 8 Final draft due	Compare/contrast essay, in appropriate genre and format, on given or chosen topic	1,000 word essay	15%
Week 9	Oral presentation based on research topic	Oral presentation	15%
Week 10 Tests	Listening Reading Writing	Test	10% 10% 5%
Teacher Observation	Students are to complete all homework tasks and readings, reflect on topics and actively participate in class discussions	Class Participation	10%

Integrated Texts:
- EAP Now! Preliminary Student's Book, Kathy Cox, David Hill, Pearson Education Australia, 2007
- EAP Now! Preliminary Teacher's Book, Kathy Cox, David Hill, Pearson Education Australia, 2007
- EAP Now! Student's Book, Kathy Cox, David Hill, Pearson Education Australia, 2004
- EAP Now! Teacher's Book, Kathy Cox, David Hill, Pearson Education Australia, 2004
- Study Skills in English. M and A Wallace. CUP.
- Study Awareness

Grammar & Vocabulary Texts:
- Academic Vocabulary in Use, Michael McCarthy, Felicity O'Dell, Cambridge University Press, 2008
- English Vocabulary in Use New Edition Upper Intermediate, Michael McCarthy, Felicity O'Dell, Cambridge University Press, 2001

Reading & Writing Texts:
- New Edition Academic Writing Course, R.R. Jordan, Nelson ELT, 1992
- Ready to Write More: From Paragraph to Essay 2nd Ed, Karen Blanchard, Christine Root, Pearson Education Inc, 2004
- Strategic Reading 2: Building Effective Reading Skills Student's Book, Jack C Richards, Samuela Eckstut-Didier, Cambridge University Press, 2003
- Strategic Reading 2: Building Effective Reading Skills Teacher's Manual, Lynn Bonesteel, Cambridge University Press, 2003
- Writer's At Work: The Essay Student Book, Dorothy Zemach, Lynn Stafford-Yilmaz, Cambridge University Press, 2008
- Writer's At Work: The Essay Teacher's Manual, Dorothy Zemach, Lynn Stafford-Yilmaz, Cambridge University Press, 2008
- Improve Your IELTS: Reading Skills, Sam McCarter, Norman Whitby, Macmillan Education, 2007
- Improve Your IELTS: Writing Skills, Sam McCarter, Norman Whitby, Macmillan Education, 2007
- Strategic Reading 3: Building Effective Reading Skills Student's Book, Jack C Richards, Samuela Eckstut-Didier, Cambridge University Press, 2004
- Strategic Reading 3: Building Effective Reading Skills Teacher's Manual, Lynn Bonesteel, Cambridge University Press, 2004

Listening & Speaking Texts:
- Contemporary Topics 1: Intermediate Listening & Note-taking 2nd Ed Student Book+ Cds, Helen Solorzano, Laurie Frazier, Pearson Education Inc, 2002
- Contemporary Topics 1: Intermediate Listening & Note-taking 2nd Ed Teacher's Pack, Helen Solorzano, Laurie Frazier, Pearson Education Inc, 2003
- Contemporary Topics 2: High Intermediate Listening & Note-taking 2nd Ed Student Book+ Cds, Ellen Kisslinger, Pearson Ed Inc, 2002
- Contemporary Topics 2: High Intermediate Listening & Note-taking 2nd Ed Teacher's Pack, Ellen Kisslinger, Pearson Ed Inc, 2002
- Contemporary Topics 3: Advanced Listening & Note-taking 2nd Ed Student Bk+ Cds, David Beglar, Neil Murray, Pearson Ed Inc, 2002
- Contemporary Topics 3: Advanced Listening & Note-taking 2nd Ed Teacher's Pack, David Beglar, Neil Murray, Pearson Ed Inc, 2002
- Developing Skills (Listening)
- Conversation Gambits, Keller and Warner. Language Teaching Publications
- Improve Your IELTS: Listening & Speaking Skills, Barry Cusack, Sam McCarter, Macmillan Edu, 2007
- Discussions A – Z, Adrian Wallwork, Cambridge University Press, 1997
- Present Yourself 2: Viewpoints Student Book, Steven Gershon, Cambridge University Press, 2008
- Present Yourself 2: Viewpoints Teacher's Manual, Steven Gershon, Cambridge Uni Press, 2008
- Passport to Academic Presentations Student's Book with CD & DVD, Douglas Bell, Garnet Edu, 2008
- Passport to Academic Presentations Teacher's Book, Douglas Bell, Garnet Ed, 2008

Suggested supplementary texts for future use in course delivery

Integrated Texts:
- 101 Helpful Hints for IELTS Academic, G Adams, T Peck, Adams and Austen Press Pty. Ltd, 2000
- 101 Helpful Hints for IELTS General, G Adams, T Peck, Adams and Austen Press Pty. Ltd, 2000

Grammar & Vocabulary Texts:
- English Pronunciation in Use Advanced + Audio CDs, Martin Hewings, Cambridge Uni Press, 2007
- New Advanced Grammar in Use 2nd Ed with answers, Martin Hewings, Cambridge Uni Press, 2005
- Advanced Language Practice. M Vince. Heinemann
- English Collocations in Use, Michael McCarthy, Felicity O'Dell, Cambridge University Press, 2005

Reading & Writing Texts:
- Critical Reading and Writing Advanced ESL Students. S Scull. Prentice Hall
- Insights into Academic Writing. M Kadesch, E Kolba and S Crowell. Addison-Wesley.
- Writing for Advanced Learners of English. F Grellet. CUP
- Study Skills for Academic Writing. J Trzeciak and S Mackay. Phoenix
- Writing Academic English. A Oshima and A Hogue. Longman.
- Writing and Presenting Reports. B Eunson. Wiley.
- Writing: Developing Skills in English Int – UpInt, Francis Manghubai, Ruth Pritchard, USQ, 1991
- Research and Referencing Course Book, Anthony Manning & Andrew O'Cain, Garnet Edu, 2010
- Extended Writing & Research Skills Course Book, Joan McCormack, John Slaght, Garnet Edu, 2010
- Studying in Australia: Editing Assignments for Content, Syntax and Presentation, M. Rosanna McEvedy, Patricia Smith, Gillian Packham, Thomas Nelson Australia, 1985
- Essay Writing for English Tests, G Duigu AEP

Listening & Speaking Texts:
- Study Speaking. T Lynch and K Anderson. CUP.
- Advanced Listening Comprehension. P Dunkel and F Pialorsi. Newbury House
- Advanced Conversation. M Giddes, G Sturtridge and S Been. MacMillain
- Listening Comprehension and Note Taking Course. K James, R Jordan and A Matthew. Collins
- Effective Presentation. J Comfort. OUP
- Motivating High Level Learners: Activities for Upper Intermediate and Advanced Learners, David Cranmer, Addison Wesley Longman Limited, 1996

Vocational/Adult Migrant Texts
- English Steps 1 Student Book + CDs, Jenni Guilfoyle, AMES, 2003
- English Steps 1 Teacher Book, Jenni Guilfoyle, AMES, 2003
- English Steps 2 Student Book + CDs, Jan Livingstone, AMES, 2003
- English Steps 2 Teacher Book, Jan Livingstone, AMES, 2003
- English Steps 3 Student Book + CDs, Jenni Guilfoyle, Paul Learmonth, AMES, 2004
- English Steps 3 Teacher Book, Jenni Guilfoyle, Paul Learmonth, AMES, 2004
- CSWE: Certificate 1 in Spoken and Written English + CDs, NSW AMES, 2004
- CSWE: Certificate II in Spoken and Written English + CDs, NSW AMES, 2005
- CSWE: Certificate III in Spoken and Written English + CDs, NSW AMES, 2005
- Understanding English Pronunciation, Susan Boyer, Boyer Educational Resources, 2006
- English At Work, Fran Byrnes, Chris Candlin, Macquarie University, 1991
- Words for Living, Helen Joyce, Macquarie University
- Words for Work, Helen Joyce, Macquarie University
- The Resume Guide: How to Write a Winning Resume, Frank Madero, New Holland Publishers Pty Ltd, 2004
- Writing and Presenting Reports, Baden Eunson, John Wiley and Sons, 1994